TAKING CHARGE!

52½ Years of Anecdotes and Advice
for Aspiring Executives

DAVE OSBORN

Taking Charge!

52½ Years of Anecdotes and Advice

for Aspiring Executives

© 2024 Dave Osborn

Dave Osborn Books
Adriel Publishing

FIRST EDITION
ALL RIGHTS RESERVED. No part of this book may be reproduced in any form or by any means whatsoever, including photography, xerography, broadcast, transmission, translation into any language, or recording, without permission in writing from the publisher. Reviewers may quote brief passages in critical articles or reviews.

Printed in the U.S.A.

Cover design by Dave Osborn and Elizabeth Lawless

ISBN: 979-8-9900885-1-1

www.DaveOsbornBooks.com

This book is dedicated to Robert M. McCollum and R. Scott Douglass, two former bosses from AT&T who taught me to lead with focus, integrity, and passion. Thanks, guys, sure miss seeing you.

Table of Contents

Forward

One of the greatest joys and scariest moments in a business executive's life is that day when the Board of Directors Chair calls you in and says, *"Congratulations, the Board has just elected you Chief Executive Officer. We are here to support you in every way and are anxious to see what changes you will make and which ways you will take us."*

As you leave the Board Room, you are excited and a bit apprehensive because the old saying – "the higher the position, the closer you are to the door" – is very true. When things take a turn for the worse, and the senior executive officer is the first one to be released. Whether it's a scapegoat move or not, it always seems to be the logical first step in a turnaround situation.

Important Notes: First, there are many ways to run an organization, and any of them will work for a finite amount of time and circumstances. What I present here is what I have learned to be the *best* model for building and sustaining a profitable organization over the long term.

Second, this book is not intended to present the entire spectrum of available knowledge on a particular topic but rather to bring a wide range of exposure in a broad scope of topics. Footnotes, suggestions, and ideas on how to learn more detail with further reading and study are included throughout the book.

I believe this guide will be useful to two audiences – first, the 30-something middle-level managers who aspire to become an executive officer, maybe even a Chief Executive Officer, at some point in their career. If you understand and can apply the principles in this book, you will stand out in your organization among your peers. You will be better prepared, and your preparation will be noticed by those who can make things happen for you. Executive recruiters will also notice you as well for career opportunities.

The second audience for this book is the new executive and/or a new executive brought into a turnaround situation whose first role is to fix something that is broken – perhaps you are already a regional or divisional general manager or executive with higher corporate ambitions. Over the many years of my career, most of my positions – and most of my career job satisfaction and rewards – have come from taking a declining or stagnant organization and moving it to an ascending business model. This book explains different ways on how to do that and then reach for new frontiers and new heights.

While some of the content in this book may seem to be basic blocking and tackling, and some of it is – no question – there are many good nuggets for any person who wants to learn more about business management from a *holistic* as well as *analytical* perspective. Alternatively, you may be new to your company and/or new to the industry and have a steep learning curve in front of you. Hopefully, this book will make your transition more organized, less stressful, and successful. Also, take time to review the footnotes as several good reading and developmental suggestions are offered there.

Good luck in your executive career development, and may you get as much joy and satisfaction from your leadership career as I did in 52+ years in the world of business.

Dave Osborn
March, 2024

Introduction

To reach the senior levels of leadership and be successful in the long term, you must be able to excel in three primary areas of basic business management.

First, you must be able to *plan and manage your organization's operations* – that's a given. It's table stakes, and you must be skilled, capable, and competent within your industry segment. You must know where your industry segment has been, where it is now, and where it is going. You must understand where your company fits into your industry segment, who and where your competition is, what your organization's strengths and weaknesses are as well as those of your key competitors. This is important whether your company has 50 employees or 500 – knowing your "playing field" – and *being known for knowing your playing field* – is the first step in moving up the corporate "food chain." Because of the wide diversity of industries and markets out there, it isn't practical to spend a lot of time in this book on managing operations. That's a discussion for another time.

The second skill you will need is to be able to *locate, hire, develop, and lead high performing people.* Somehow executives develop the thought process that as you move up the ladder, you can do it all by yourself and that people will instinctively and automatically respect you and your position to follow you to the ends of the earth. While this may be somewhat true in the military, for the most part it isn't true in the civilian workplace – particularly in the post-COVID world we live in now. Also, remember that employees may respect your position because of its authority but may have reason not to respect *you*. That's a problem, and we will spend some time on how to develop those leadership skills that so many executives either don't think they need as an executive or simply don't think enough of their people to develop.

KEY THOUGHT

More executives fail because of leadership and people skills – *or lack of them* – than with deficiencies in the financial or operating areas.

The third skill you will need at the top is to be able to *think and plan strategically and manage capital*. Strategic planning and managing money sounds fairly simple, but it gets complicated in a hurry. If you expect to grow your company as an executive – or fix it if your company is in trouble – you're going to need a good strategic plan and more money available to you beyond what you receive each month just for paying the bills and meeting payroll. You're likely going to be looking for money to fund internal, organic growth as well as to fund potential acquisitions. You will need to understand what an investment banker can do for you, what it means to take money from a private equity group, and how to invest your company's financial assets prudently and properly to achieve the greatest return. Knowing the numbers and what they tell you is vital in an executive position, and unless you are coming up through the ranks in accounting or finance and have a CPA, your financial background probably is inadequate for an executive position. My early career was spent in technology sales and sales management. I was a whiz at figuring pricing, margins, commissions, and discounts, but with important business ratios that would tell me what I need to be doing – not so much. I had to make a conscious effort to shore up my financial acumen when I took on General Manager and, later, Chief Executive Officer responsibilities.

KEY THOUGHT

Master the fine arts of managing operations, leading and developing people, and strategic thinking and planning while properly managing capital, and you will be ready for an executive title and a corner office.

Part I:

Hiring, Leading, and Developing Your People

Chapter 1:
Precious and Scarce Resource

The first rule of leading and developing people is to value them as a precious and scarce resource. Many businesses think of employees as necessary evils that must be hired and are, for the most part, expendable. They tend to hire with low expectations and are never disappointed. Their attitude is that employees are basically interchangeable commodities who will do as little as possible to collect a paycheck – and they treat them accordingly. The reality is that without good people, your business will fail over time. It may take months, or even years, but your business will deteriorate unless you truly value your employees and act accordingly.

Getting and keeping employees engaged in the organization's business is vital. I spent my entire career in telecommunications and broadband services which is very capital intensive and highly automated. Many of the larger, national companies in this space have long ago closed down customer service centers, laid off technicians, and exported their technical support overseas – all in the name of cost control. The problem they now have is that they can no longer be responsive to their customers – their needs or their wants. Their employees are not valued as in previous years and, not surprisingly, are much less engaged than in times past. This lack of employee engagement shows up in all facets of their business and creates customer churn, dissatisfaction, and poor customer reviews. I spent my last two decades in a regional broadband company which was *highly* focused on its customers. We offered all the online features and functions, but people still enjoy talking with people so we made it a point to staff local offices and offer personal and friendly service. It made a huge difference in our sales and customer satisfaction.

Our geographic service area is known for hurricanes, and we had a bad one every 2-3 years with minor ones more frequently. I remember with Hurricane Dolly in June, 2008, how we were back up and fully operational within 4-6 hours after the rains stopped. Now to contrast that recovery scenario, had we lost our *people*, it would have taken *months* to stabilize our business, and we would have lost many, many customers during that time. The recent pandemic gave us a little taste of what that would be like. With schools and businesses closing due to the pandemic, students and workers started working from home – and of course that meant beefing up their broadband services at home. Our demand for services went up 40% during the pandemic, and we constantly had to deal with technicians being exposed to a COVID-positive person and then quarantined for up to two weeks. So with a 40% increase in demand and an average of 15-20% of our techs off the job being quarantined at any given point in time, our service installation intervals slipped out from 1-2 weeks to 5-6 weeks. It was an awful experience, but it solidified my conviction that a business cannot be a successful business without good, loyal, engaged, and well-managed employees.

KEY THOUGHT

The message here is that an executive must have a genuine concern for the organization's employees and be sure they get everything they need to do their jobs well. The role of an executive as a leader is to provide direction, resources, and a supportive environment where employees can become fully engaged and highly motivated to achieve the goals and objectives at hand. Said another way – *you must have a heart for people to succeed in the long run.*

Chapter 2:
Management and Leadership "Styles"

Many books have been written over the last few decades about management and leadership styles. They are available for your reading pleasure on Amazon, Microsoft, Goodreads, and many other sources. Many of them are tied to formal assessment vehicles that typically categorize leaders by their assertiveness and analytical orientations. These are all great tools to learn more about yourself and how you might react to certain situations or circumstances, but they really don't often give you much practical advice on growing as a leader and executive. The term "practical advice" to me has always meant – what am I learning that is actionable, *i.e., what will I do differently next Monday morning when I get back to my office?* I learned that if I couldn't translate the training theory into day-to-day action back on the job, the training content would never become useful to me.

One of the more actionable management style grids I have seen is not new – it was originally developed decades ago but is still very relevant and applicable in today's world. It is the Robert Blake-Jane Mouton[1] grid developed by two professors at the University of Texas in Austin. It maps *concern for production* against *concern for people*, i.e., the organization's employees. While our focus here is on senior management, the Blake-Mouton grid and philosophy can apply from the boardroom to the mailroom.

The grid looks like this:

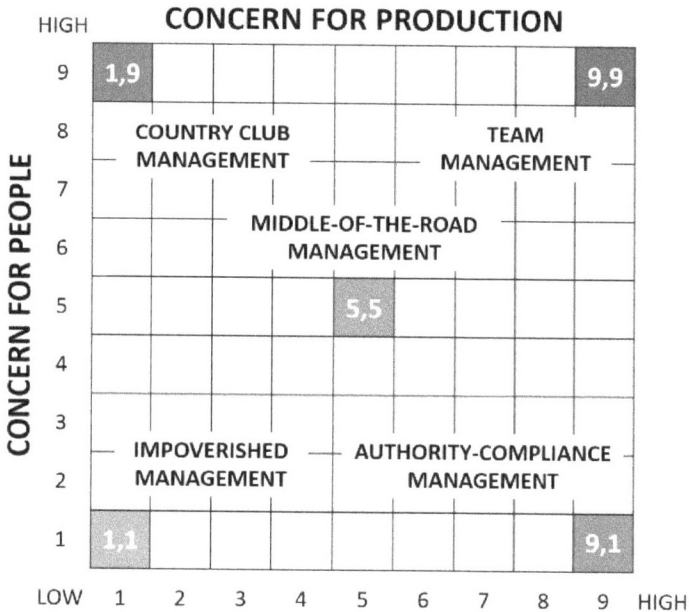

Key: *The axes on the grid are concern for production and concern for people respectively. The numeral "1" indicates low concern while the numeral "9" represents a high concern. The first numeral represents production; the second numeral represents people.*

Various management styles according to the Blake-Mouton Management Grid studies:

The "9/1" Manager

The 9/1 manager is the "authoritarian dictator" who cares only about production at the expense of concern for people or relationships. This environment is usually always a lousy place to work. People are taken for granted and viewed solely as a resource. Engagement and loyalty are low, turnover is high, and production is rarely optimized – no matter how much the boss threatens and yells at the crew. The objectives will usually always be met, but the workplace will always be a sweatshop. Innovation is non-existent.

Another problem with 9/1 leaders is that their peers typically don't like them any better than their employees do. Peers often have to "work around" a 9/1 leader because he/she missed a deadline or opportunity because one of their employees got fed up and quit at a critical time. 9/1 types tend to stand out in an organization and not in a favorable, positive way. You will find a lot of 9/1 types in the military – and they typically move up the ladder *with a high cost to their units*. During the sales and sales management phase of my career, I had way too many of these types of bosses, and I was always glad to get transferred away from them.

Because they are solely focused on production, the 9/1 manager, when faced with sagging profitability typically takes the easy way out and moves to cut costs rather than to improve revenues. Since payroll and its related expenses are usually well over half of the average organization's expenses, they are quick to lay off and furlough employees. While this may obtain a short term benefit, layoffs typically lower customer service and care *unless the organization's business model is fundamentally changed to operate as or more efficiently with less people.* Typically this does not happen – employees are simply terminated to lower costs and obtain better profitability while service levels deteriorate, service quality suffers, customer satisfaction suffers, and customers find other providers. The 9/1 manager often will mortgage the future of his/her organization to achieve a quick turnaround without pursuing improving sales and obtaining new customers.

The "1/9" Manager

The "1/9" manager is the "country club" manager who cares about people, relationships, and a positive work environment at the expense of production. This organization is focused on being a friendly environment and easy tempo but can never reach its potential and will be lucky to keep the doors open. Predictably, the turnover rate is low, and the employees love to come to work! Feedback and growth is minimal in this environment.

You will often find a 1/9 manager in a government position or a non-profit where results are not measured in the conventional manner. The goal of 1/9 management is stability and maintaining a pleasant work environment. When these types of leaders get into the business world, they will typically not be found in key leadership positions but rather in support and other less visible roles. They are out of balance with their needs for approval and are still focused on being liked at any cost.

The "1/1" Manager

The "1/1" manager is the absentee "impoverished" manager who isn't concerned about either people or production. This organization will develop a lazy, unmotivated workforce that will work when they get around to it with little or no commitment or responsibility. This organization will not thrive, nor will it stay in business long. The "1/1" organization can make a great acquisition target.

The classic "1/1" manager is a long time employee who knows there are no more promotions coming and they have another 10 years to retirement. His/her plan is to do as little as possible and leave early as often as possible. Mentally, the "1/1" manager has checked out of the organization and is just marking time and taking up space.

The "5/5" Manager

The "5/5" "compromise" manager tries to strike a balance but can't do a good job on either production or relationships. This leader will absolutely not rock the boat and will avoid confrontation at all costs. The organization will usually get by, but it will live in mediocrity and never become an industry leader or achieve any great successes. Most organizations tend to fall into this category.

A typical "5/5" manager usually comes in two varieties. The first is a support role like human resources, warehouse management, or accounting and finance. In addition, you will also see a lot of these in middle management in larger companies. They were successful in the lower levels of leadership, but when they got to middle management or a little higher, they lost confidence in their ability to get control of their responsibilities. You will find long term managers with little or no career movement ahead that are similar to the "1/1" manager only they are a bit more engaged. These situations are similar to the familiar Peter Principle in that good supervisors could not make the performance jump to manager or executive. You also see a lot of these in sales where the best salesperson was promoted because of his/her outstanding results but then didn't like the supervisory, coaching, or mentoring responsibilities and did not perform them as needed. Sales and sales management are two very different jobs, and success in one does not guarantee success in the other.

The "9/9" Manager

The "9/9" "integrative or team style" manager is where Blake & Mouton want to go with leadership – *high* concern for *both* production and people. This manager is a strong leader that can deliver results while developing a strong employee team with a good balance of trust and development. This organization will have high employee engagement, high loyalty, and exceptional production achievement. This organization will become an innovative environment with direct and immediate feedback. In the "9/9" organization, you will find that heart, passion, and concern drive the following:

- Innovative, engaging feedback
- High performance

- High expectations
- Direct feedback
- Real time feedback
- Support from above
- Advocacy from all directions

The "9/9" manager has it all together with a perfect balance of their supervisor, peer, and subordinate needs for approval along with a genuine focus on developing their people to achieve at a higher level. If the organization's culture is a positive environment, there are likely to be several "9/9" managers. I was fortunate to have numerous "9/9" managers throughout my career, and these leaders made me look forward to Monday morning and returning to work.

Chapter 3:
The Employee Performance Model

Early on I learned from a great boss[2] that optimal employee performance comes from an adequate combination of motivated *knowledge, skills, and ability.*

Knowledge in this context means whether a job candidate has the education, training, or experience to do a given job. This will vary all over the map according to the responsibilities of the position to be filled. Some entry or lower level positions will not require much knowledge at all while higher level positions might require advanced degrees, certifications, and other relevant training or experience to meet the needs of the job. It's been my experience that many times too much attention is paid to a candidate's academic or training accomplishments rather than their workplace experience.

> *Knowledge answers the question – does the candidate have the education and training experience to handle the position at a highly competent level? Does he/she have sufficient knowledge needed to meet the needs of the job?*

Skills in this context refers to how well the candidate has mastered the duties to be performed on the job. If the job to be filled is a cable splicer, how well can the candidate splice? Do their splices look strong, clean, and professional? If the job is a merger and acquisition specialist, how well can the candidate perform financial analyses? How well can they research and analyze industry trends that will influence a purchase or sale price? You get the idea at this point – it isn't just that the candidate knows *what* to do, but rather they know *how* to do it, and they can they do it *well enough* to satisfy the needs of the job to be filled? Skills are more important for good performance than most people give credit. Too often candidates are selected for positions based solely, or least primarily, upon their academic and training accomplishments with little or no attention paid to whether the candidate can *apply* their education and training to accomplish a task. I have found this to be true from the mailroom to the boardroom.

> *Skills answers the question – does the candidate have the work experience and on-job experience to handle the position at a highly competent level? Does the candidate have sufficient job experience and competencies needed to apply their knowledge to meet the needs of the job?*

Ability in this context is fairly straightforward – it is whether the candidate simply has the intellect, physical talent, and/or energy to get the job done. This can be very hard to assess for upper level positions without a diligent, detailed, and thorough hiring process. This characteristic also tends to be fairly binary – you either have it or you don't. If you do, you do, and if you don't, you aren't likely to get it.

Ability answers the question – does the candidate have the mental, physical, and/or emotional capacity to handle the position at a highly competent level? Does the candidate have sufficient "smarts" to meet the needs of the job?

These three important components that form the cornerstones for performance – *knowledge, skills, and ability* – are much like a three-legged stool. By way of comparison, with a four-legged stool, you can be minus a leg and the stool can still stand – maybe a bit wobbly, but it can stand. The three-legged stool is very different because you have to have all three in place or the stool will fall over. If one of the legs is missing – or short – the stool will collapse, and the candidate will fail.

So how do you prevent a candidate from failure? Glad you asked – read on.

Chapter 4

The Employee "Life Cycle"

Every job candidate hired by an organization goes through an employee "life cycle." All that means is that there is a beginning, interim assessment points, and a final assessment and evaluation which restarts the cycle for another round. If the components within the life cycle are executed correctly, the odds favor the success of the candidate in the position. When candidates fail, it always seems to be traceable back to a mistake or omission of one of the life cycle steps – or stages. The stages of the employee life cycle are as follows:

- **A Well-Written Job Description.** Every position in an organization should have a thorough, detailed, and current job description. Job Descriptions are often ignored or done hurriedly for appearances; however, they are extremely important during the hiring process because they:
  - ○ Form the basis for a clear understanding of exactly what duties the employee is expected to perform and what responsibilities the employee will have;
  - ○ Provide an objective basis for performance evaluation;
  - ○ Provide the basis for the establishing performance standards, e.g., goals and objectives, enabling the objective documentation of performance improvement

or adverse employment action should the employee fail to perform.

Duties and responsibilities should be as detailed as possible in job descriptions. Granted there will always be that last 10% "other duties as assigned by the supervisor," but realistically, this shouldn't be more than 10-15% of a position unless it is a part-time job, intern, or some other lower level position whose primary function is basically to be available when needed. I have learned over the years that the better and more detailed the job description, the better the selection process will go.

- **Recruiting.** Recruiting should be focused on *finding candidates* and should be more than just putting an ad online in one of the many job hunting websites and job boards. Recruiting starts with knowing *where* to look for the best candidates for a particular position. Just as you go to certain geographic locations to hunt for certain species of game or go to certain bodies of water to fish for certain species of fish, you look for good candidates where they are most likely to be. Do your research, and don't expect to find a good senior level position candidate by running an ad in the local Sunday paper. Expect to use industry association contacts, executive recruiters, and networking with your peers to find good senior level people.

As you move down through the organizational ladder, the recruiting methods change. Candidates for lower level positions are typically younger and are looking for a job as opposed to looking for a strategic career move. Recruit accordingly.

- **Selection (Testing/Interviews).** Interviewing candidates is usually ineffective because the interviewer is not trained or skilled at interviewing. They usually don't know exactly what they are looking for, because they don't have a well-written job description, so the questions will not obtain the desired information. If the interviewer will focus on questions that reveal and establish *knowledge, skills, and ability,* the results will be more useful.

KEY THOUGHT

It has always amazed me that organizations will hire – and then fire – a six-figure executive or manager who wasn't a good match for the job because they would not spend $150 to learn about a candidate's suitability or fit for a position.

Ask questions about academic and training curricula – the *whys* and *hows* of their achievements. Ask questions about particular jobs or assignments the candidate's resume states and delve into how decisions were made, how problems and failures were dealt with and resolved, and how employee problems were resolved. What was the value that was delivered and the tangible outcome to the organization.

To learn about the candidate's abilities, several good testing instruments are available for a modest fee that will give not only some insight into a final candidate's mental acuity but also their "fit" for a particular position.

In addition to being interviewed by upper-level managers, candidates should also be interviewed by employees that will be peers as well as employees that are a level lower than the candidate. This is known as a "360" Interview, and candidates may behave very differently interviewing with different levels of the hiring organization. It is often very interesting to compare notes after the employee leaves, and it is a red flag is when a candidate interviews differently at each level.

It cannot be overstated how important it is for more than one person to interview job applicants. People tend to be drawn to people similar to themselves and will tend to favor an applicant with whom they feel a connection – even if other applicants are better qualified. This is called the "doppelganger effect." A "doppelganger" is a reflected signal – also a twin – which mirrors the transmitted signal. People tend to hire people that are like themselves – it is human nature, and multiple interviews and review discussions can minimize the effects on hiring.

- **Hiring.** Once a hiring decision has been made on a final candidate, an offer letter should be sent in a timely manner. A 2-3 week lag between the final interview and the offer letter tells the candidate that there wasn't much urgency to the hire and that they are not filling a critical or key position - regardless of where it is on the organizational chart.

This is not a good impression to make with a new employee that you want to become highly engaged and vested in the organization's success. It also tells the new hire that there is lots of bureaucracy in the organization that they will have to deal with. The offer letter may also be returned because the candidate has received another offer during the wait time and got tired of waiting on your organization to extend an offer. To counter this, prepare ahead of time and send the offer letter as soon as possible.

The offer letter serves many purposes besides a title, salary, benefits, and start date. The offer letter should also contain – depending on the state – references to at will employment, union membership alternatives if appropriate, and other such legal notices. Employment contingencies such as pre-employment physicals and drug testing should also be included.

While the offer letter needs to address some important legal areas, most attorneys will tell you that sometimes "less is more" when it comes to itemizing every single employment legal issue that may or may not be relevant. Unless the offer letter accompanies an employment contract, the best path is usually to keep it simple.

- **Company Induction.** Once a candidate has accepted the offer and met any required contingencies, he/she then will become a new employee. How new employees are treated during this process will start to form their opinions of just how good an organization they just joined – and it needs to be a positive experience. The first day is, depending on the size and scope of the organization, usually spent with Human Resources filling out a pile of forms to get the new employee made aware of and enrolled for health care, dental care, vision care, group life insurance, long term care, 401K, direct deposit for payroll, tuition assistance, etc. Each takes some explanation and should properly be related to the value of these benefits.

This is a great time to be sure the new employee realizes that these benefits are worth *another 30-40%* on top of their new salary. This is the first exposure the new employee will get to the culture of their new organization. It can either be a positive or negative experience depending on how it is conducted. Most employers do not fully understand or appreciate this step and view it simply as "getting all the paperwork out of the way." Employees rarely forget their first day with the organization. It is extremely important that this be a good experience for the new hire. The importance of "onboarding" cannot be overstated, and it is the hiring manager's responsibility to ensure a good experience with the induction processes.

- **Job induction.** Once all the forms have been signed, the new employee is released by Human Resources to their new supervisor or manager. The best way for the hiring manager to get a new employee engaged quickly is *not* to say "Go get'em, Tiger," but to spend some time orienting the new employee to the work area and work group.

To become fully engaged, a new employee needs to understand what role his/her new department plays in accomplishing the organization's objectives. Further, he/she needs to understand how their particular work group contributes to the departmental objectives and how each employee contributes to the work group's success.

Whether the new employee is running the mailroom or a division, he/she needs to know from the beginning that they are essential to the organization and its success. He/she needs to know where he/she fits in and how his/her contribution moves the ball down the field to the goal line.

These early days of employment are critical – if the new employee is made to feel he/she is important and he/she fully understands his/her role in the organization's success, he/she will not only become engaged but will become a leader. Organizations tend to omit or overlook this phase from middle management on down – which is shortsighted as this will be the bulk of the workforce. If an organization has employee engagement issues, this is a key place to review first.

- **Manager/Supervisor Oversight (Personally or by Assignment).** A new employee – depending on the place on the organizational chart – should have oversight fairly frequently during the first few weeks or months. This may be daily at first, then as needed. Later a simple weekly check in or a chat during lunch – or it could be a formal work review like a weekly status meeting. During this period, the hiring manager should also ensure that the new employee meets and has one on ones with all key stakeholders – again commensurate with the scope of the new employee's responsibilities.

This is where the new employee continues to learn and adapt to the organization's culture and get a deeper understanding on what is expected on the job. It's hard to give a new employee too much help and feedback during this period.

KEY THOUGHT

Feedback is key at every level. it can be daily or weekly, formal or informal – it doesn't matter so much how or when, but rather that it is being done.

Some supervisors or managers may delegate these activities to a subordinate as a developmental exercise. As long as the new employee is getting competent, useful, and constructive feedback, the organizational position of the feedback giver is less important.

• **90-day Evaluation (Depending on Job Level).** Some positions, e.g., most hourly employees, some first level supervisors, and some professional contributors such as engineers, accountants, sales representatives, and customer service representatives, have rather quick "ramp up" times based upon personal accomplishments and should be ready for some sort of formal feedback and evaluation at the 90-day point. It doesn't need to be lengthy or fancy – it just needs to be real time, competent, focused, useful, and constructive. These new employees are still in the early stages of their employment and need to know where they stand after the first 90 days. Reviewing the employees' performance at the 90 day point usually ends with a few tweaks instead of major developmental issues.

It is important that managers keep new employees on track and correct issues in real time. The further off track the new employee gets, the larger the journey they will make *together* to get back on track.

- **180-day Evaluation (Depending on Job Level).** As you move up the organizational chart, the ramp up times tend to increase. Supervisors and managers typically fall into this category along with other individual contributors e.g. attorneys, auditors, lobbyists, etc., and are ready for feedback at the 180 day point. Again, feedback at this stage, with this audience, should be largely about focus, priority setting, and following organizational practices in addition to the actual performance of their job duties.

- **1-year Evaluation (Depending on Job Level).** Upper level positions e.g., officers, vice presidents, C-level executives, typically take a year or two to master. While feedback along the way is constructive, most of these positions usually require making strategic, personnel, and long term operational changes which take longer to implement and demonstrate the results of the changes.

Feedback at this level should be written and detailed, leaving the incumbent with no doubt as to the senior view of their performance. Correspondingly, corrective measures should allow for a reasonable timeframe to correct. Unless the organization is fairly small, major changes may be difficult to make quickly.

The decisions at these various stages of the life cycle will be basically pass or fail with different outcomes depending on the employee's place in the organization and the organization's desire to retain and further develop them.

If the assessments are favorable, the best course of action is usually to continue the employee's development and begin to assess their ultimate potential within the organization. Successful employees can be given more responsibility in their current assignments, given more complex assignments, and/or given mentoring responsibilities to develop other employees.

If the employee has less than the optimal education for the position, e.g., lack of pertinent college or graduate degrees, certifications, or professional credentials, this is the time to initiate those additional goals. If the employee has potential beyond their current position that might require those additional credentials, this would be the time to discuss that with the employee and see what commitments are willing to be made to achieve them.

Additionally, potential leaders can be "rotated" through various positions at their level of management. This is routinely done in larger organizations that have numerous positions at each level of management. The more rotational assignments a leader gets, the better prepared they will be to assume the additional responsibilities at the next higher level of management. Job rotation is an excellent training tool and should be implemented if at all possible in your organization. I was rotated many times[3] while working for a large company, and I found each new assignment an opportunity to learn more about the business from a different perspective and appreciate the broader view of the organization gained from these experiences.

If the evaluation is a "fail," then it is likely that at least one of the steps in the employee life cycle was omitted or done poorly. The underperforming employee's life cycle should be reviewed to determine where the employee life cycle process broke down. Once the probable cause has been identified, the organization should, first, correct the deficiencies in the employee life cycle process so that this failure does not recur. Following that, the root cause of the employee underperformance should be researched and determined according to the employee life cycle performance model and identified as a *knowledge* deficiency, a *skills* deficiency, or an *ability* deficiency.

If the deficiency is determined to be *knowledge*, then the employee may need to be retrained or need additional training or education. A knowledge deficiency usually means that the employee did not have an adequate education or training to competently perform the required job duties. These may have been internal candidates who were promoted too quickly or new hires who did not perform well in their education or training obtained elsewhere. The first decision is to assess whether the employee wants to improve and is, otherwise, a good employee you want to retain, or whether you should cut your losses and terminate employment now.

A *skills* deficiency determination usually means that the employee's past experience elsewhere did not adequately provide the work experience to master the tasks of the position. Remediating a skills deficiency can be fairly straightforward in some positions and very difficult in others. I have found that sales and customer service skills can be improved fairly quickly with role play, coaching, demonstrations, and the like. Improving skills in the technical areas is more complex because the root cause of the skill deficiency may be from not following instructions, working too quickly, not checking the work prior to leaving the job site, or lack of attention to detail with reports and record keeping. These are as much attitudinal issues as skill issues but need to be addressed as a single deficiency.

If the evaluation determines that the failure is an *ability* deficiency, most of the time it is game over for the employee in this position. As an employer, you have two choices – if you like the employee's work habits and engagement, then you might find another position within the organization that is a match for the employee's ability. Failing that, the remaining option is termination of employment. And while this sounds like a viable option, it indicates that management failed somewhere in the hiring process.

KEY THOUGHT

Never forget that failed employees did not put themselves into their positions but rather management. A failed employee indicates a need to improve the hiring process – starting with the application of the core principles of the employee life cycle.

On terminating employment: Terminating employees should be a painful task. If it is not painful, you probably should not be leading or supervising people. There is nothing worse you can do to a person – other than taking away their life – than taking away their livelihood. As stated earlier, when employees fail, it is usually because management made a mistake or miscalculation somewhere along the line. Performance failure, for other than negligence or deliberate action or inaction, is usually as much the leadership's fault as the employee. That said, parting should be done with compassion. The best thing you can do for an employee whose employment you have terminated is to get that person employed somewhere else by doing whatever it takes to help accomplish that. The benefit for the employee is that their financial situation does not deteriorate too badly. The benefit for the employer is that the terminated employee is off the street and earning a living again and won't be inclined (or have time) to post negative comments on Facebook or LinkedIn or seek the counsel of an attorney.

Chapter 5
Performance Appraisals

Probably the job duty managers hate most is writing appraisals. Most managers would rather walk through hot coals or get a root canal than close their door and write annual appraisals of their employees. It's not that they don't know what they want to say – it's just writing a good appraisal is a tedious process that most managers put off and off until they rush through it without a lot of thought. From my experience, the biggest problem managers have with writing appraisals is:

1. There is no up to date useful job description to provide objective performance benchmarks containing goals, objectives, and values contained within the scope of responsibilities.

2. They have avoided giving an employee corrective feedback periodically during the evaluation period, so the evaluation's criticisms and resulting corrective action will come as a great surprise to the employee.

3. They have not documented their employees' work performance and only have vague generalized recollections of what they want to tell the employee.

4. They simply can't remember enough to give meaningful feedback to the employee.

5. They know when the appraisal has been delivered, the employee will say, "Why didn't

you tell me I wasn't doing the job like you wanted? I could have improved if you had told me."

When I would receive a request to approve an employee termination for performance, the first words out of my mouth were always, "Bring me the last two appraisals and any other incident documentation you have on the employee you wish to terminate. Also, bring me the improvement plan or plans you gave the employee to improve their performance prior to coming to a termination decision." And as you already can guess, I rarely got anything useful back from these requests. This created some angst along the way, but I've been through both state unemployment challenges and wrongful termination litigation, and it isn't fun to have your management team raked over the coals because of inadequate feedback, inadequate documentation of performance, or a lack of corrective action plans. If there are surprises in an evaluation, the appraising manager has not done his/her job. It is really that simple.

Writing appraisals is much easier if the manager has done his/her job and given feedback and corrective measures along the way. It is part of the job necessary to grow and develop employees – and arguably one of the more important parts of a manager's job. Usually the appraisal process consists of a "continue – start – stop" format that addresses "*continue* doing this, *start* doing this, and *stop* doing that." While this format usually works at the hourly and first level supervisor positions, it is insufficient for mid-level employees and up. In giving feedback and performance evaluations for this audience, I have found that it is useful to:

- **Focus on what is *next*.** Once the employee has been made aware of a marginal or less than satisfactory rating in a particular area, the real issue is what happens next? Identifying a problem is fairly straightforward, the remedy maybe not so much. The manager should always have an idea of what is needed to resolve a failure to meet fully satisfactory ratings. How will the manager do that? Refer back to the guidelines for knowledge, skills, or ability. If the manager is not completely sure, the manager should ask for help from Human Resources, a peer manager, their boss, whatever. Never give an employee bad news without a plan to fix it.

- **Focus on what will be *different*.** Many times in my early career in sales management, I would be reviewing a young sales representative's performance who was not meeting his/her quota requirements, and he/she would always say, "boss, next month I will work harder and close twice as many sales and make my numbers." When I would ask how they were going to do that and what did they mean by "work harder," I would get a blank look in return. I would then ask what they were going to do *differently* the next month to get a *different result*. At the end of the day, everyone knows that if you keep doing the same thing, you will get the same result, so to get a different result, you will have to do something different. The sales representative could not close more sales without a) having better closing skills or b) having more prospects and presentations at his/her current closing ratio. So since the rep could not a) materially improve his/her closing skills in a single month[4], he/she would need to b) make more cold calls, set more appointments, and make more presentations. That would actually make sense. Point being – to obtain a different result, something different will have to happen in the subsequent evaluation period.

• **Don't "sandwich" criticism.** Managers have a tendency to give good news, then bad news, then – oh, yes – back to good news. This wastes time and confuses the employee who is listening and thinking "I'm doing OK, I'm not doing OK, but I'm doing OK." I always considered it demeaning when I would get appraisals like that, and I promised myself never to do that when I gave appraisals later on. Employees are (for the most part) grown adults and should be treated as such. If the employee has a problem with some aspect(s) of his/her performance, you have to get it out on the table in the open to deal with it. The employee has to understand *completely* that the deficiency is an issue that *must* be corrected or it might become career or job-affecting at some point in the future. Sugar-coating negative feedback with a "compliment sandwich" simply won't get the job done and serves neither the employer nor the employee.

* **Give the employee the benefit of the doubt.** Always assume the employee wants to do a good job and to improve until they show you otherwise. Not all employees can be great communicators, and their responses to your appraisal will vary from employee to employee. Some outgoing employees will respond enthusiastically and promise to do better while other employees will go silent and not know what you want them to say. This is another reason why managers simply must give feedback more than once during an evaluation period. The smart manager *will be giving feedback continuously* – both supportive and corrective. Small, short, weekly comments will be helpful and won't create the emotional response that an annual appraisal will. The sooner feedback is given, the less painful and the better to get on track quickly.

Another reality in giving appraisals is that some people just don't like each other but have to work together. On many occasions managers will have a personal bias against one or more of their employees for a number of reasons. It could be a personality clash, different political opinions, ethnic differences, an expensive university education (or lack of it), or some other prejudicial opinion. It might be excessive absences to care for a chronically sick parent, spouse, or child. The point being - a performance appraisal should always be reviewed by another manager familiar with the employee being appraised. It might be a manager one level up, a peer manager, or even a *former* manager. An objective performance evaluation must be free of whatever prejudices the appraising manager might have. Never forget you are dealing with people's careers, and appraising managers have a moral *and legal* obligation to appraise and evaluate performance fairly and honestly.

• **Avoid focusing solely on weaknesses.** When we talk about giving appraisals, managers instinctively go into a "fix it" mode. You may have an employee that excels in many areas and is a good strong "B" player except for a couple of deficiencies. The manager will typically spend most of the appraisal time talking about improving weaknesses regardless of how small or immaterial they are in the grand scheme of things. To use a sports analogy, let us say you have a golfer who doesn't have a lot of distance on their drives but can chip and putt quite well. Don't spend all your time on gaining distance, but rather spend as much or more time getting the chipping and putting up to a professional level.

KEY THOUGHT

The old golf saying, "You drive for show, but you putt for dough." Is very true indeed. Point being – pay as much attention to improving areas in which an employee is excelling as you do to fixing deficiencies. That is what is called solid, well-rounded employee development.

In overseeing an entire organization, it is important to benchmark disparate work groups with a common performance standard and should include:

- **Job performance**. How well did the employee do in achieving their goals and objectives for the year? How well did the employee do in staying within their expense budgets? How well did the employee do on special assignments and unusual requests?

- **Behavior**. How well did the employee do in adhering to the organization's standards for behavior with regard to showing respect, not bullying, no harassment of any kind, and civility with fellow workers?

- **Contribution.** To the betterment of the organization. What did the employee do to improve their job in terms of improving the job's practices, procedures, efficiencies, cost reduction, time reduction, etc.?

In order to assess and evaluate behavior, a special type of evaluation tool is needed. A variation on the traditional job-oriented evaluation method is a valuable developmental tool I learned from Don Leach, a fellow manager at AT&T. He called it a "quotation review;" however, I have also heard it called a "360 review." What Don would do with his direct reports is get three sheets of paper and go through the office and simply ask people what the first thing that came to mind when the manager's name was mentioned. One of the sheets was for managers one level up, the second for peer managers, and the third for managers one level lower. The results were always interesting and spoke volumes about the employee's reputation and level of respect within the organization. It takes a competent, experienced manager to conduct a quotation review, but the output can be very useful at reinforcing or modifying a manager's behavior. I personally found great value in this process in developing leaders within an organization.

Banding and ranking. Once all the employees are evaluated, they are typically rated within "bands" – usually numbered or lettered typically on the order of:

- Greatly exceeds expectations
- Exceeds expectations
- Meets expectations
- Meets most expectations
- Does not meet expectations

This is why a good job description is important – so that all assigned duties and responsibilities are included, and that the evaluation and appraisal covers the total job. From this point, the usual outcome is stack-ranking and wage treatment if justified. In some larger organizations, the lower stack-ranked (the bottom 10% for example) employees are discharged. While this might be a viable short term strategy with an acquisition or the takeover of a failing organization, it eventually ends up being counterproductive once an overall level of competency and expertise has been achieved.

Non-standard evaluations. Sometimes a performance evaluation and appraisal is about more than employees. On terminating relationships in general, I learned the following over many years and many experiences:

Sometimes you have terminate *customers*: No organization can please everyone – it's just not possible. Sometimes, it actually makes good business sense to terminate a customer and refer them to another company that maybe can meet their needs. From a list of examples of this, one of our broadband customers didn't like paying his bill and was suspended for non-pay over 50 times in a five-year period – that's almost every month. He would always call in and complain that our service was bad, he couldn't access it, and that he wanted a credit for all the times he couldn't use the service, etc., etc. He even wrote the Texas Public Utilities Commission, then the Federal Communications Commission, then his Congressman complaining about his service, how we wouldn't give him fiber (he was several miles from our fiber network) and so forth. Once I sent this customer's payment history, these government staffers would quickly let the matter go. Finally, when he was suspended for non-payment of his bill, we elected not to reconnect him. I wrote him a "good bye" letter, and that was the end of the situation. When I reflected on the countless hours of our customer service, network, and technician staff this customer wasted, I kicked myself mentally for not terminating his service earlier. Profitable customers are good for business, unprofitable customers not so much. They waste time and money and should be released in a professional manner.

Sometimes you have to terminate *vendors*: In a capital-intensive business like telecommunications and broadband, vendors are everywhere. An interesting thing that happened some years ago was during the evolution mentioned elsewhere of the transition from a legacy switching equipment environment to modern soft switch Ethernet technology. Of just under ten vendors in that market space, only one – Nortel – had manufactured legacy equipment. Almost all of the soft switch manufacturers were startups with little or no track record – just some really slick equipment. With our industry service standards of 99.999% uptime (that equals to about six seconds per year downtime), doing business with a startup for core network equipment was considered quite risky. We looked at financials monthly to be sure the new companies were profitable and selected a vendor in New Hampshire that looked very promising. We really liked our account manager and all the founding executives. We even visited their factory in New Hampshire and got assurances of their quality control and the competency of their technical staff. We bought their equipment and installed it in all our offices.

We rocked along for about a year, then we started hearing rumors that they were burning cash and not doing well. Our vendor's CEO made the trip down to our offices to reassure us, but I told our Network Manager to get a contingency plan just in case. We started shopping again and ended up switching to an alternative vendor platform just as our New Hampshire vendor declared a Chapter 11 (reorganization) then shortly thereafter a Chapter 7 (dissolution) bankruptcy. If we had not "fired" the original vendor we would have been left with abandoned equipment with no upgrades, firewalls, security updates, and the like. Sometimes you have to leave a good vendor that you really like to keep your business safe and secure.

Chapter 6:
Assessing Potential

The first thing to know is that assessing potential is very different from evaluating performance, and I learned not to do them at the same time. They need to be done separately because a performance evaluation is, or should be, fairly *objective*, while assessing potential is, by its nature, somewhat *subjective*. Another thing I learned is that while I could do appraisals on my own, I needed my colleagues input to help with assessing potential. This is because getting my colleagues thoughts and opinions:

- Helped to cancel out some of the built in bias I might have regarding the employees long term potential for any number of reasons;
- Gave a different view of perspective of the employee's perceived strengths and weaknesses from other people's vantage points; and
- Provided some ideas on what would be a good development plan to prepare the employee for more responsibility.

One thing to remember in assessing potential is that you need to have a good, clear understanding of what you want in your leadership team. Managers often think they know what they want in a leadership position but haven't really given it enough thought. Leadership positions in different departments with different skill sets can have very different needs when it comes time to select leaders. An interesting anecdote to ponder on this topic is the way the famous French military leader Napoleon assessed his officers. He created a grid that measured *intellect* and *energy* in order to learn which traits were most important and most desirable in his officer core. It looked like this:

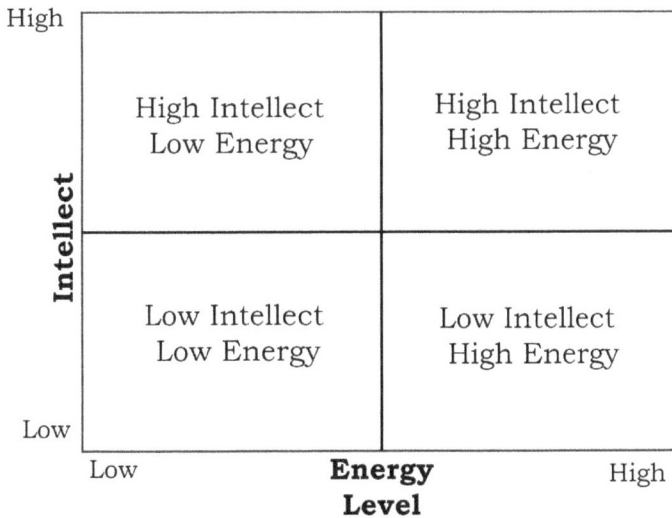

	Low Energy	High Energy
High Intellect	High Intellect Low Energy	High Intellect High Energy
Low Intellect	Low Intellect Low Energy	Low Intellect High Energy

Intellect (vertical axis: High to Low)
Energy Level (horizontal axis: Low to High)

Napoleon then evaluated each of his officers and was surprised at the results. In terms of which quadrant would hold the most effective and most desirable officer, he expected the "high intellect, high energy" officers to be his most desirable and best officers – and he was correct. In understanding the least desirable officers, however, he automatically assumed that the "low intellect, low energy" officer would be the least desirable officer to have. To his great surprise, he discovered that the "low intellect, low energy" officers didn't accomplish much, didn't initiate much, and didn't rush onto the battlefield unprepared. On the other hand, the "low intellect, high energy" officer rushed into battle, often without thorough and proper planning – and got men killed.

Napoleon learned that his *most valuable* officers were the high energy, intelligent officers, and his *least desirable* officers were his "energetic dullards" as he called them.

KEY THOUGHT

High energy doesn't always equal great potential. When assessing the potential of your workforce, it is natural to look for the go getters that have a lot of movement, a lot of activity, and stir up the pot to get things done.

Be sure you know what you want in a position before you fill it. Be sure to look beyond these obvious traits and assess both their *results* and their *"casualties"* along the way. Did your hot shot candidate make his or her numbers but caused other departmental employees to quit or transfer? Did you lose a few customers with over-aggressive account management? If so, you may want to hold up on moving that person up the food chain and do an in depth assessment of how valuable they really are to the organization's long-term success. These people usually make terrible executives because they got there for the wrong reasons.

Another concept to consider in assessing potential concerns how the manager being assessed develops people. Long ago as a freshman in college, I learned an important sociological principle:

Ontogeny Recapitulates Phylogeny

This is more than just a catchy phrase. "Ontogeny recapitulates phylogeny" is the foundation of something called recapitulation theory. Recapitulation theory supposes that the development of individual organisms (ontogeny) follows (recapitulates) the same phases of the evolution of larger ancestral groups of related organisms (phylogeny). Basically, what all this means is that "like begets like," i.e., dogs will have dogs, and cats will have cats. The business application here is that leaders will almost always build and develop people in their own image because that's the one they are the most familiar with. If there are *any* concerns with the character, priorities, behavior, ethics, morals, values, whatever, of the manager being assessed, you are going to eventually see the same issues to varying degrees in their subordinates. Think long and hard about promoting people with character deficiencies – the chances for long term success are limited.

This is also good time to get introspective and think about your own career and where you see yourself going. You start with your career goals – which should factor in to every position you accept in your organization. For example:

- If you are in a large company and already know you want to move up to an executive position, you should be doing everything possible to achieve that goal. That means you have (or will obtain) the *right* education, the *right* experience, the *right* mentoring, the willingness to relocate, and access to the right opportunities. If you see a path forward within your current organization, then it makes sense to stay with the organization, gain experience, build your network, and work toward an opportunity to advance.
- If you are in a smaller company where the person in the job you want is only two years older than you are – or they are the son or daughter of the owner – you are probably going to have to change organizations to get the position and experience you want. If you are in this position, you should work the industry associations to make senior contacts in similar companies who could use you, and also network for contacts with executive recruiters who work within your industry.
- If you are not sure of what you want, then it only makes sense to keep doing what you are doing and build a reputation for extreme competency and helpfulness. Regardless of your final career choice, you will be well-grounded for advancement at some point.

On numerous occasions, I have been asked "what about lateral moves that are not promotions?" Should I take those or hold out for promotions?" My answer is usually to take the lateral move if it is a different job and broadens your base of experience. Experience typically makes you more valuable, so a lateral move to broaden your experience can certainly be career enhancing. As mentioned earlier, when I was a mid-level manager at Southwestern Bell, I took several lateral moves to gain experience. As I was finishing up my MBA at TCU in Fort Worth while working in the Dallas office, I accepted a lateral move to St. Louis General Headquarters to be a product manager in the marketing department. I was very excited to have a headquarters staff job to apply my newly acquired knowledge. Not only did I enjoy my job, but I met several influential executives as well as their key managers. The Vice President of Marketing was a Scouting executive, and, since I am an Eagle Scout, I was asked to join his St. Louis district council committee to help out with camping events. He took a liking to me and always stopped by my office for a quick chat when he was in my building. I also got to know the top executives in the eight operating areas in SWBT's original five states and all the key people on their staffs. I also made several business trips to AT&T headquarters in New Jersey and New York which brought me new contacts and colleagues there as well. You see where I'm going with this – it's not just the job but the business contacts you make along the way with lateral moves that, if you do your job well, can help with achieving your career goals.

Chapter 7:
Leadership and Management Concerns

Congratulations, you just got promoted to a new leadership position. You've always wanted to be a boss and enjoy the pay and prestige that accompanies a leadership title. Your goal is to be the best boss ever – *the boss you never had.* You're going to be loved and respected throughout the entire organization for your strong leadership and employee engagement.

You just fell into the first pitfall of being a new leader.

Leadership Needs for Approval

Employees in leadership positions have three particular "needs" in their leadership role – the need for *boss* approval, the need for *peer* approval, and the need for *subordinate* approval. They are *all* important and must be *in balance* in the long term to optimize a leader's performance. The need for approval is like a pie (see the charts below) because it you make one slice bigger, the other slices have to be smaller. There is only so much pie to go around, and if you make one need bigger, the other needs get less pie.

Figure A
New Supervisor
Needs
For Subordinate
Approval

Figure B
New Supervisor
Needs
for Boss Approval

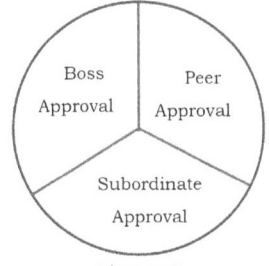

Figure C
Supervisor Balance of
Needs

Take a closer look at the need for boss approval. This is natural – you just got the new job and want to show your new boss that their decision was a good one. You want to do a good job so you can keep it and perhaps get another promotion down the road. Working for primarily your boss's approval is often referred to as "managing upwards"

What often happens, however, is that you are promoted to lead and supervise your former teammates. You are now supervising the workers that were formerly your peers and who know all your strengths and weaknesses. You used to sneak off with them to the movies, shopping, watering holes, going home early – whatever – and now you're responsible for their production and productivity. *But* – you want to be the boss you never had so getting their approval and respect in your new role is important and is a high priority for you (Fig A). You now develop a high need for *subordinate* approval, and, over time, it is human nature for your former teammates to take advantage of you. You don't hold them as accountable as you should because you want to be the best boss they ever had and be respected and regarded as such. It is natural for results to trail off, and the group's performance will show it. As your need for subordinate approval grows, it reduces the other two needs – that for your peers and your boss – and at the one year appraisal, you get rated lower than you hoped because the results have trailed off.

Now, having gotten a mediocre or less than satisfactory first year rating, the pendulum swings the other way to make pleasing the boss the top priority – and the need for subordinate approval drops off dramatically (Fig B). Your employees won't know what hit them when you start dropping the hammer and demanding that they perform and holding them accountable for their performance.

The goal is all about balance (Fig C), and it's about this time that you decide whether or not this supervisor thing is really what you want. The good news is that once balance is restored to meeting the organization's needs, things can rock along on an even keel for an indefinite period.

The need for *peer* approval is interesting and was a problem for me in my early career years. In fact, it was specifically mentioned to me with a warning after a two-day management potential assessment I attended early in my career. In larger organizations where there is more structure and there are numerous supervisors at each "level" in the organization, it is very common for ambitious people to ignore or even hold disdain for their need for *peer* approval. This was me, and I tended to look at my peers as potential competitors for promotions, and I viewed my peers as the "enemy" who could take my well-deserved promotion away. Experience taught me that this was a *huge* mistake – and one to *must avoid*.

I learned that larger organizations have an endless need for leadership people, and when you do get that promotion, you want good people to take with you as you move up the organizational ladder – and your former peers will be those people. It works the other way around as well, in that if your peers get promoted before you do, and you have been a supportive peer, they will bring you up the organization with them. In short – your peers can be as important to your moving up the organizational ladder as the leadership currently in place. And yes, some of your peers will turn out to be ineffective and untrustworthy, but those situations tend to work themselves out over time. Very, very few leaders with these traits make it to the boardroom, and most are eventually thrown under the bus by their peers.

KEY THOUGHT

Your peers report to the same people that you do and are often alone with them without your presence. Their access to leadership can either work for you or against you – it's all in how you treat your peers. If you treat them poorly or exploit opportunities to make yourself look good at their expense, they will indeed become adversaries who will take delight in shooting you down in front of the senior management team. Many promising executive careers have stalled out because peers did them in. If, however, you can see your peers as allies and support them, help them, and foster teamwork, you will build career-long colleagues and advocates.

Chapter 8
Getting Things Done

I have seen talented managers fail in their positions because they did not get all their tasks completed and their key objectives achieved. While there are several variables in this endeavor, the primary reason for their inability to achieve their goals was their inability to manage their time effectively. They would always tell me they were too busy, they were overwhelmed, they had too much "red line[5]" time, too much time with subordinate issues, and so forth. It was never mentioned that the *successful* managers had all the same side issues to deal with but were *still* achieving their goals and objectives.

At the heart of the problem, the unsuccessful manager was unable to properly schedule and manage his/her time. Robert McCollum, as mentioned earlier, taught me a great lesson, and that was how to build an Annual Job Plan. This sounds very simple, and while it can be complicated, it is very straightforward, fairly simple to construct, and will be a valuable tool in getting the job done.

Here is how to build an Annual Job Plan:

    1. First, have an up to date, accurate, and complete job description for your position which outlines *all* the duties and responsibilities you have in your position. This will give you some overall direction on what to be sure to

include to build a work schedule for an entire year.

2. Set up an Excel spreadsheet with 12 columns that represent the months January through December with a "total" column on the far right – a 13th column. The rows down the left side will contain all the activities and things you have to do during a typical year. Remember that some of your activities, e.g., annual budgeting, business conferences, appraisals, vacations, etc. will be occasional – *or even annual* - activities rather than monthly activities and will only show up in a few months or even a single month.

3. For each activity on the left side of the spreadsheet, now enter in each month's cell how much time you plan to spend on each activity, then total it in the 13th – or "annual total" column. For example, if you plan to hold a two-hour staff meeting each Monday morning, that would be – for most months – an eight-hour entry. You can handle the exceptions by entering 10 hours in four months to give you 52 weeks. If you won't be holding meetings over the end of year holidays, you might just be entering 10 hours for *two* months – you get the idea. The total should be 50 or 52 times two hours per week for the weekly staff meeting for a total of 100 or 104 hours for the year.

4. Continue to do this with *each* activity on *every* row until you have mapped out the

number of hours per month you plan to spend until you have completed the spreadsheet. The more granular you can get with the estimates, the more value this exercise will have for you. Also, if you get interrupted with customer complaints, service outages, weather issues, executive requests, etc., look at your current year calendar for your history, then be sure to estimate how much time you are likely to spend on these "red line" items in an average month for the following year. Typically, the totals on red line time leave managers in a state of shock and disbelief when they see how much of their time these non-productive items take.

5. When you have the monthly and annual numbers for all activities – including the red line time – for all 12 months, your Annual Job Plan spreadsheet is complete, and it's time to analyze it.

What you will almost always find is that while each year contains 2080 hours of "normal work week" time (e.g. 40 hours per week for 52 weeks), you have likely "over planned" your time by as much as 100%. This is an important part of this exercise, and you now have some idea why you're not getting anything done and why your projects and goals are not being met. Unless you do something different, you will have the same result each and every year. The only way you can succeed now is to "reprogram" your time to prioritize and focus on your *key goals and objectives*.

How do you go about that? No one said this would be easy, but some workable strategies include:

1. **Delegation.** Many of your activities can be delegated to your subordinates and could be excellent for developmental purposes as well as getting some of these less important activities off your plate. Things that can easily be delegated are meetings you attend, reports you have to submit, certain business trips, some coaching or other project oversight – plus these also make great developmental opportunities for your people. Much of the "red line" time can likely be delegated to subordinates as well.

2. **Reassignment.** Perhaps your peers could take over some of your activities. If you attend weekly or monthly gatherings for Rotary Club, Lion's Club, and United Way, perhaps some of your peers would benefit from taking over some of these responsibilities and broaden their horizons. You say you've been a Rotarian for 10 years and don't want to give it up? Sharing the opportunity and getting your job under control trumps that.

3. **Just Don't Do It.** Do you really need a two-hour staff meeting every week or would a 30-minute "tailgate" meeting suffice? If you're following any of the many good time management programs, meetings are one of the first things they limit, shorten, or eliminate. Learn to use email or text messages – you just don't need people around a table than often for that long. You will find it

amazing how many things you can just stop doing and no one will notice and production will not suffer.

The reality, though, is that even after slashing your activities to what you consider an absolute minimum, you will probably still be left with a 50-55 hour work week average. You will, though, have much greater odds of meeting your annual goals and objectives than you did before. Also, a lot of your estimates were based on current year history, and if your service problems get better and the weather cooperates, you might even under run your estimates.

KEY THOUGHT

The first year will be the hardest – after that, somehow it becomes easier as you learn to focus on what truly moves the ball down the field and achieve your goals and objectives.

I have since learned about several other methods to manage time that you may want to Google and learn about and review. Check out the following:
- The Pomodoro Method
- 2-Minute Rule
- 1-3-5 Method
- Eisenhower Matrix
- Pickle Jar Theory
- Task Batching Technique

Chapter 9:
Establishing Corporate Values

Sooner or later the question comes up – what about our corporate values? We need to have a set of corporate values! You can't be a successful company without corporate values – right?

What should you do?

The problem facing a leadership team with developing their corporate values is that most of the time, they wind up with all types of motherhood and apple pie cliches.

- Excellence?
- Respect?
- Integrity?
- Customer Care?

These components are usually expectations and typically show up in some variation in value statements – which is nice and makes everyone feel good, but they are not really worth much because:

- They tend to create a cynical atmosphere with employees who work there every day and know these values aren't honored;
- They don't do much to *differentiate* your organization. The more motherhood and apple pie statements you adopt, the more you sound *like* – not *different from* – your competitors.

Most organizations typically make three mistakes when they set out to establish a list of their corporate values:

- Their value statement consists largely of common traits that every successful organization embraces. The corporate values developed will usually be what you *want to be* rather than *what you are*. This does nothing for your particular company, and your employees won't pay much attention to them.
- Executives turn the value statement development over to Human Resources which, in turn, tends to make the process a group activity with employee input, etc. The result is consensus mush that doesn't challenge your employees or mean much to them. There can be no vision for the organization without executive involvement and direction.
- The rollout of the corporate value statement tends to resemble a marketing launch campaign with a rollout, lots of attention, then little or no follow up.

Our first efforts at a corporate values statement started out exactly this way, but we quickly saw that there was no component for change or challenge until we changed our mindset and focused on incenting action and challenging the employee body.

So why have a corporate value statement? The real answer is that people just think they have to have one but have no idea how to develop one. If you want corporate values that mean something, they should, when revealed, make some of the employees *uncomfortable* because they require *commitment*, *accountability*, and *performance* in order to comply with them.

KEY THOUGHT

Corporate values should set a clear benchmark on what it takes to be successful in your organization.

Developing corporate values is difficult and is a job for the executive team, *including the CEO*, and some of the key employees. They should, as a team, discuss what has made your organization successful, what has made it a great place to work, and what sets you apart from your competition. That could take several weeks, if not months, to complete and should specify in simple terms the basics of how to develop the mission, vision, and values with:

- Development of *true values* vs. expectations and wishes;
- Defining the *mission* of the organization being the "what" you want to accomplish;
- Defining the *strategy* of the organization being the "how" you will accomplish it.

Then, once a meaningful list of corporate values is developed, it needs to be baked in to every facet of your company's organization at every level in every department or division. Communicating your corporate values needs to be an integral part of your:

- recruiting and onboarding process,
- employee appraisal, recognition, and award processes, and the
- employee termination process.

Sometimes it would be better for an organization *not* to develop a list of their corporate values because having no corporate values would be healthier than having corporate values that everyone knows are window dressing.

But – *if* you are willing to put in the time and effort and do it right, a meaningful set of corporate values can be inspirational and a guiding light for employees and the leadership team[6].

Chapter 10:

Employee Engagement in the Workplace

Are your employees engaged in your business? How can you tell? Employee engagement is defined as the extent to which your employees are committed to making the business meet its objectives, but study after study shows that employees are, for the most part, *not* fully engaged in the business but rather report to work each day to see what will happen.

A high level of employee engagement in your organization's culture is important because if you don't have it, your organization is functioning with literally one arm tied behind its back. You are paying employees a fair wage and getting $.50 on the $1 dollar for your investment.

How do you achieve a high level of employee engagement? To start, develop your management team to the "9/9" manager level on the Blake-Mouton grid, and you will see engagement begin to move in a positive manner.

There are several schools of thought on improving employee engagement:

The **"five pillars"** of employee engagement are:

- **Communication.** Keep your employees informed. If you don't do so, the rumor mill will take over, and that's never good. I never saw a rumor mill that portrayed management in a good light.
- **Learning and development.** Offer opportunities for employees to grow personally

and professionally. Offer opportunities for career development and tuition assistance for university education that supports the employee's current skills and position.

* **Autonomy.** Offer some control of their destiny to make employees stakeholders in the success of the organization.

* **Work-life balance.** Don't make your workplace like the Dilbert cartoon`. If you're going to need 24/7 coverage for something, make a schedule, pay an on-call bonus, and then leave the other employees alone. Refrain from texting or emailing at 11pm unless it's a true emergency.

* **Recognition and rewards.** Study after study tells us that employees appreciate recognition as much as they do a raise. Recognition costs nothing and has a profound impact on employee morale and commitment – which leads to higher levels of employee engagement. Rewards can be simple – trophies, plaques, parking place next to the door, whatever – it doesn't matter as long as there is recognition and appreciation included in the process.

Then there are the **"Five C's"** of employee engagement:
* Care
* Connect
* Coach
* Contribute
* Congratulate

Do you see a pattern here? The end game is *"one dream, one team.*

KEY THOUGHT

Any organization can achieve a high level of employee engagement if they follow the first rule of the Blake-Mouton "9/9" leadership – placing a high level of value on their employees and communicating to them respect and appreciation. If you truly value the employees, make it a key part of your duties each day to talk to employees and encourage them in any and every way possible.[7]

Chapter 11:

Accountability in the Workplace

During my career I took over several organizations that were in trouble, i.e., not making their numbers and/or not delivering a quality product or service to their customers. What I found in most of these circumstances was that the previous leader had not been the classic 9/9 manager but had been a 1/9 or a 5/5 manager. Telltale signs of the 1/9 and 5/5 leadership styles are the absence of accountability in their organizations.

> **KEY THOUGHT**
>
> **Holding people accountable is not rocket science – nor is it the 9/1 manager's crack a whip over the heads of the workers to get the production goals met. Accountability is simply holding people to their word that they will get things done.**

Accountability starts with getting buy in and commitment from an employee that a project will be completed with quality results on a certain date given certain resources. The next step is to periodically follow up to be sure progress is on track. When an employee says, "Gee, boss, I got the info from engineering a week late, so I won't be able to make the deadline," a good response might be, "OK, what is your next step to get it done? When are you going to do that? Can I count on you for that?[8]" A larger issue here is that the employee failed to hold the engineering department accountable and was now trying to pass the failure off as an "oh, well, you know how it goes with engineering."

To hold employees accountable and build a culture of accountability, you must:

1. Set the expectation with new hires that timely work completion is an expectation and a requirement for continued employment in your organization. Then follow up on a regular basis.

2. Set clear goals to be achieved along with the expectations for their accomplishment. It is a good idea to put this step in writing to be sure the scope of the undertaking is understood. The task doesn't necessarily have to be reasonable, but it does have to be achievable.

3. Follow up and get and give regular feedback. This should be frequent at the onset and should discuss the employee's progress to date and expectations for the next week, month, etc. If there are potential problems on the horizon, the time to identify them is *when the corrective action is a tweak rather than a major course correction or a failed commitment.*

4. Keep track of the progress being made by the employee. You will need a record for performance evaluations and appraisals later on. This is the documentation that is invaluable for improvement initiatives. The old saying, "you inspect what you expect" is never more true than within this context.

5. Be consistent with all employees – say what you mean and mean what you say. Don't go easy on one employee and not expect the others to notice and take note. This will affect future behavior – count on it.

6. Work with other departmental leaders to reinforce each other's accountability goals. Accountability won't become part of the culture unless it becomes the "norm" for expected behavior throughout the organization. The illustrative comment earlier about engineering always being late is symptomatic of accountability in one area but not another.

Here's a great quote from management guru Peter Drucker on accountability:

"If your goals are larger than your need to be liked, you will reach your goals. If your need to be liked is larger than your goals, then your goal will become the need to be liked."

There is also a great December, 1999, *Harvard Business Review* article by William Oncken, Jr. and Donald L. Wass called *Management Time: Who's Got the Monkey?* I recommend reading it as a guide to helping create a culture of accountability. The article illustrates how employees will essentially "delegate upward" with a dialogue that goes like this:

Employee: "By the way, Boss, we've got a problem here. You see..."

Boss: (not wanting to give an answer on the spot) "So glad you brought this up. I'm in a rush now. Meanwhile, let me think about it, and I'll let you know."[9]

They then go on about their business, but who has the problem now? The problem has successfully been delegated upward, and little or no accountability remains with the employee. A better answer to the employee might have been, "that's interesting. Think about it and give me three alternatives on how to fix this. We can discuss it tomorrow in our staff meeting (or whatever)." You can't build a culture of accountability without holding people accountable for their work. It's that simple.

Building an organization with a high level of accountability is not easy[10], but it is worth pursuing until you have it in place. Once it's in place and part of the culture, all things will become easier, faster, and more consistent. Production, service, and morale will soar!

Chapter 12:
Trust in the Workplace

Stephen M. R. Covey wrote a great book[11] on trust in the workplace, and I recommend that you read it cover to cover. It's a fairly easy read that will go quickly and deliver an important message.

Essentially Covey begins by telling us that there are two kinds of trust:

- I can trust you to do what you say you are going to do. When you tell me you are going to do something, I can take that to the bank. **(Dependability or Character Trust)**
- I can trust that when you say you are going to do something, that you have the knowledge, skills, and ability to accomplish the task at hand. **(Competence Trust)**

This chart[12] lays the trust foundation out quite well.

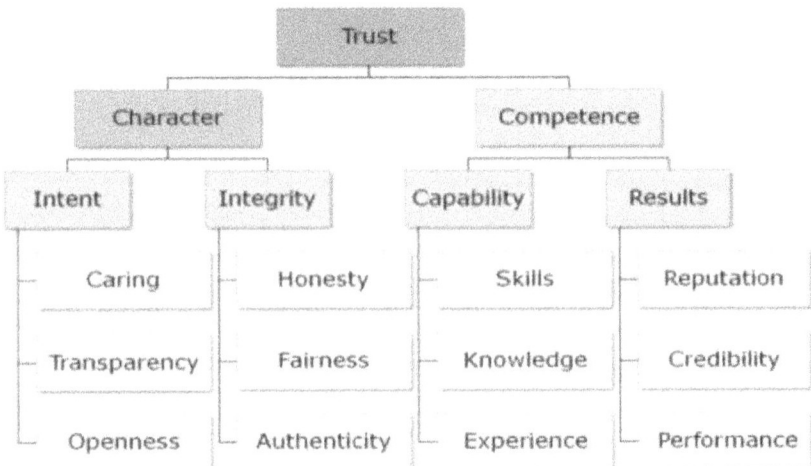

Trust			
Character		**Competence**	
Intent	Integrity	Capability	Results
Caring	Honesty	Skills	Reputation
Transparency	Fairness	Knowledge	Credibility
Openness	Authenticity	Experience	Performance

Who needs trust in an organization? *Everyone* needs trust in one manner or another. When there is high trust in an organization, people can work on verbal instructions, text messages, emails, and so forth – and things will get done on time and on budget. The pace of this business is fast and efficient because people know their backs are covered and they won't be left hanging in the wind.

If the organization has a low trust culture and environment, people will *not* act on verbal requests and instructions but will wait on a paper trail to protect themselves and their work groups. They will *not* move forward until they feel secure that they will *not* be hung out to dry by people that do *not* follow through. The pace of this business slows to a crawl.

Covey calls the "high trust" environment one with a "trust dividend" because the high trust environment enables agile and quick responses to customer needs and demands – which leads to growth, customer satisfaction, and prosperity. In contrast, Covey labels the "low trust" environment as one with a "trust tax" because sales and profit dollars – and often customers – are lost due to the lack of action while employees are waiting on paperwork to cover their butts.

How long does it take to *gain* the trust of your coworkers – both up and down the organization chart? It takes *repeated demonstrations* of your meeting commitments and achieving results. Remember, trust is more than just keeping your commitments, it's also about delivering the qualitative results you promised. Building trust can take months or even years depending on the position you are in.

How long does it take to *lose* the trust of your coworkers? You can lose it in an afternoon if things go south and you can't fix it.

KEY THOUGHT

Trust is hard to build and easy to lose. Never forget that. How do you maintain your trust? You make it your most important goal to deliver on time and on budget and let nothing get in your way.

It is important to mention intellectual honesty in this context. What is intellectual honesty? The first time I heard the term "intellectual honesty" was in an appraisal given to me many years ago in Kansas City by R. Scott Douglass, one of my most respected managers at AT&T. Scott told me I had intellectual honesty, and I had to ask him what that meant. It is simply being true to yourself. Never lie to or kid yourself; never lie to others. If you hit a roadblock, don't tell yourself that something will somehow come along to fix it – in other words, don't tease yourself that things will somehow work out without making a change somewhere. The classic definition of insanity is doing the same thing over and over and expecting different results. Recognize when you need help, fess up and get help. Never let your ego rule and keep you from seeking help and assistance to complete your task on time and on or under budget. You have to know what you know and know what you *don't* know.

Once you have achieved a high trust environment and culture in your organization, you are well on your way to a healthy, productive organization. The three-legged stool of a healthy, productive organization means that:

- Employee engagement is in place
- Employee accountability is in place
- Employee trust is in place

Once you have these three key items in place, you and your organization will be in the best possible position to face the future with whatever challenges and opportunities it may present.

Chapter 13

The Need to Embrace Change

We are living in fluid times, and continuous change has become the norm.

I believe change is, by and large, misunderstood. There's an old saying, "No one likes change except a wet baby." But I think that statement oversimplifies it – people *love* change to get a *new* car, *new* clothes, a *new* house, *new* shoes – well, you get the idea. It's not about change *itself* but about understanding the *need* for change, losing *control* of or leaving behind a process you are familiar with and having to learn a *new* one, and perceiving a *personal benefit* for yourself. Let's face it, at one level it's all about "why do we have to do this" and "what's in it for me?"

Change requires something called "cognitive flexibility." Cognitive flexibility is simply the ability to learn *and the ability to unlearn*. Change requires both – giving up the *old* way and learning and mastering the *new* way.

I once attended an excellent training seminar on organizational change given by Dr. Jerald M. Jellison, a really knowledgeable change expert from the University of Southern California whom I enjoyed getting to know. Jerry is a long time professor of psychology at the University of Southern California and has written four books about implementing and managing change in organizations[13].

Dr. Jellison designed a very inciteful graphic called the "J-Curve" to illustrate the five phases of change:

J-Curve Model

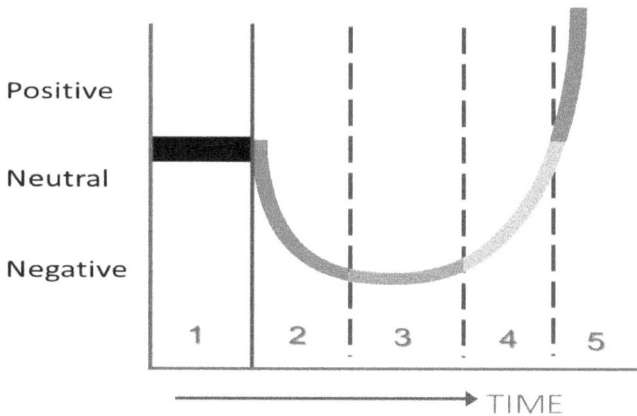

- **Stage 1 is "The Plateau."** At the beginning, before the new effort gets underway, employees are at a performance plateau. Before the actual change begins, they're following established patterns. They often have a high degree of mastery of the work. And, even if they aren't masterful, they're comfortable with the routine. They've got their time-honored ways of dealing with customers, procedures, equipment, and colleagues – and they're sticking to them. "We've always done it this way" is a common refrain at this juncture.

Once the news of change is announced, reaction to the news will vary, depending on its perceived effect. Some will see opportunity and embrace it. Others will see possible loss of stature, position, or relevance and start a quiet resistance movement. During this stage, there can be *fear* of the unknown or simply fear of a bad outcome for the worker. Fear then gives way to *anger* and *resentment* about a possible loss of position, power, authority, whatever, followed by *self-doubt*, that is doubt that the new system will work better than the old one or that the worker won't be able to cut it with the new rules or system. This is very normal and is to be expected in a major change project.

- **Stage 2 is "The Cliff."** The second stage begins when employees, many feeling as if they've got a gun to their back, step into the abyss and actually try to start doing things the new way. Maybe this means using new software, reporting to a different supervisor, learning to operate a new piece of equipment, adopting a new procedure, or the first meeting with your counterparts in the firm that just acquired yours.

And, of course, what happens when we do something that is radically different from what we've done in the past? Performance drops sharply. The Stage 1 pattern is reversed – failures now outpace successes. This is not surprising, as anyone who has taken up a new sport can attest. The novice skier falls a lot, the fledgling golfer shanks into the rough, and the new fly fisherman snags every tree branch within range.

When workers begin to do something new and different, their performance cannot help but drop. As the problems accumulate, you hear: "I knew this would happen," "It's only going to get worse," or my personal favorite, "We're doomed." As the thoughts turn more negative, so do emotions. A sense of failure can permeate the workforce, and everyone wants to escape and return to the old way of doing things.

At this stage there will be many mistakes made, and it is important to "celebrate failure." This simply means to learn from the mistakes and not dwell on them or punish for them. If the employees can "fail fast," they can make mistakes, learn from them, then quickly move on.

- **Stage 3 is "The Valley."** As employees enter Stage 3, things start bottoming out. Errors aren't as frequent or as large, and workers are starting to do more things correctly. As they begin to master, for example, some of the basics of the new software program, they gradually complete more tasks successfully. They still make mistakes; however, they tend to catch them and correct them quickly. This is the stage during which you can observe the transition that takes place between the old and new ways of doing things.

As Stage 3 progresses, workers begin to achieve some consistency. As successes begin to now outnumber failures, employees turn cautiously optimistic. Although still not brimming with confidence, they think, "Maybe I can, sort of, do this."

- **Stage 4 is "The Ascent."** In this stage, performance improves impressively. The curve rises almost as rapidly as the earlier descent. Why? Because the workers sharpen their skills, establish new procedures, eliminate inefficiencies, and coordinate better with each other. Not only are they doing things better, but they're getting a psychological boost from their newfound proficiency.

Employee attitudes about the new way of doing things changes dramatically as their performance climbs in Stage 4. You now hear employees say, "This isn't so hard," "I'm better than I thought I was," and "I think I can actually figure out a faster way to do this."

- **Stage 5 is "The Mountaintop."** Finally, in Stage 5, performance now matches and then *exceeds* the old way of doing things. Workers are now proficient in the new way of doing business. During this stage, performance continues to shoot upward as success piles upon success, errors are virtually eliminated, and costs are reduced. Change has been achieved.

Such achievements validate our beliefs in our own capacity to deal with challenges. "This old dog can still learn a few new tricks," and "Why did we wait so long?" are typical of comments heard during Stage 5.

When Jerry was explaining the J-Curve, he emphasized that change over some period of time was not just one big J-Curve, but rather a series of smaller J-Curves along the way. This makes perfect sense as different departments go through the change process at different rates and have successes earlier and later accordingly. What actually happens looks more like *this* graphic where you have a *series* of drop-offs and recoveries.

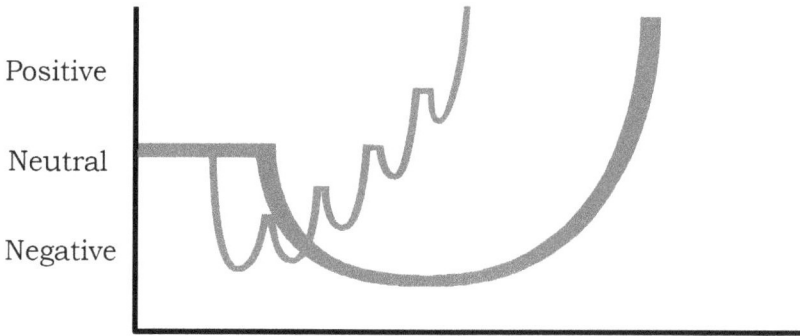

So, why do we need to endure all this constant change? Let's pause for a moment and review that.

The first, and primary, reason organizations need to change is because the industry they were in constantly evolves and can look very different over time. Many influencing factors – technology, education, political events, international competition, and weather, to name a few, are continuously changing the landscape. Successful organizations understand this and bake it in to their culture and planning processes. They learn to embrace change and keep their focus on their customers like their organizations depend on it because they do.

The following is common knowledge[14] regarding technology, but it bears reviewing:

- **Netflix** did not kill the movie rental business – ridiculous late fees did.
- **Uber** did not kill the taxi business – limited taxi access and fare control did.
- **Apple** did not kill the music industry – being forced to buy full-length albums to get a single song did.

- **Amazon** did not kill book retailers – bad customer service and experience did.
- **Airbnb** isn't killing the hotel industry – limited availability and pricing options are.

Never forget that technology by itself will not be the *real* disruptor – not being customer-centric will be the biggest threat to your business. In the examples above, each of them resulted because the organization stopped listening to their customers. If the organization can build and sustain a "customer obsession," it will be better positioned to adjust to meet the changes in their marketplace.

There is a book written years ago called the Power of Positive Thinking[15]. It puts forth the premise that to accomplish something you have to think positive thoughts. That is a great start. Jerry Jellison puts forth the *Power of Positive Doing*. It is very simple, and we can all do this every day:

- First, focus on one small goal at a time. Don't try to solve all the problems in an afternoon.
- Next, define steps at ground level. Keep it simple and remember that the best ideas usually come from those closest to the work.
- Remember that a lapse is not a relapse. If something goes wrong, it's not the end of the world. Don't get discouraged, just fix whatever broke and move on.
- Finally, create opportunities. Every employee has an opportunity to improve our company in some manner. In our company we constantly polled our employees for ideas to adapt and

complete tasks faster, easier, and for less cost. We were never disappointed.

Having been through 52½ years of constant radical change in telecommunications, I learned firsthand that the best path is consistent and open communications combined with frequent interaction with the affected employees. If you meet with the resisters early on and often, they will become adopters. Change also becomes a bit easier when employees don't feel isolated or less valued than before the change process began.

As the group enters Phase 5, the change will be recognized as being worth the effort, and over and over again I have actually heard people say – "we should have done this 10 years ago."

Reducing the *time* during the change process will also reduce the *cost*, so it pays to reward the early adopters. When other employees see the early adopters rewarded for their role in affecting change, the incentive will be there for the next change. Create an environment where the first employees to accept change "win." This will lower the costs of change going forward.

KEY THOUGHT

Change is inevitable in today's world. Embrace it and make it work for you.

I've been asked, "What do you do with an employee that just won't change or embrace the change?" My answer is always the same – give them time. Like Jerry said in his change model, the resistance doesn't come because the employee doesn't like change. The resistance comes because the employee fears failure with the new way after success with the old way. Training, more training, coaching, and regular follow up and encouragement will mitigate all but the most stubborn workers. Eventually the resistance subsides, and life goes on. For the most stubborn 1-2% of the workers, there are two remaining options: if they are good workers, find them another position within the company. If they are less than an ideal workers, a strategic outplacement is likely the only reasonable course of action.

Chapter 14:

Reporting to a Board of Directors

Sooner or later you may report to a Board of Directors. I can tell you from experience that the only thing more difficult than having a boss, is having 7, 8, 9, or 10 "bosses" sitting on a Board of Directors.

Boards are different in every organization and have very different make ups depending on whether the organization is public or private, large or small, or for-profit or non-profit. The job of the Chief Executive in this case is to keep all the board members on the same page with the same priorities. This is not easy.

- **For-profit** boards are generally composed of executives who have been asked to be on the board because they offer some benefit, e.g. they are commercial bank executives, attorneys, investment bankers, executives of major customers, and other similar business relationships. As a rule, the directors have extensive business experience and can serve as a valuable mentor and advisor to the CEO and the organization's executive team in general. They are paid for their service and are highly respected in their respective occupations and positions. Their focus is solely on maximizing opportunities for the organization, which they view as their highest priority.

- **Non-profit** boards can be very different. Most of the time these positions are not paid positions and are essentially a form of community service. The most typical of this type of board would be a school board or the board of United Way, the Better Business Bureau, the local food bank, or some other similar organization. The directors typically know little or nothing about running the organization at hand and depend on the organization's CEO, or Superintendent in the case of a school board, for managerial expertise and leadership. My experience on the boards of the Better Business Bureau, Texas Telephone Association (TTA), Texas Lone Star Network (TLSN), Texas State Telephone Cooperative (TSTCI), and WTA – Broadband Advocates was been that this type of board is a great way to give back to your community and industry as well as to network and meet other key executives in your market area. I consider my 17+ year service on the Houston-South Texas Better Business Bureau Board to be one of the great experiences of my entire career.

Like for-profit organizations, some non-profit organizations ask people to join their board. Alternatively, however, many non-profit boards such as school boards and boards of utility cooperatives have publicly elected positions for some set term. An issue that often arises with publicly elected directors, though, is that they often view their primary loyalty to be to those who *elected* them rather than to the best interest of the *organization*. Unlike members of congress, however, publicly elected directors do not "represent" their electorate per se but rather were *elected to do a job* and should view their primary loyalty to be the organization and *not* to their "constituency." Directors, regardless of how they obtained their position, have a fiduciary *and legal* responsibility to their organization that surpasses all other concerns. Creating policies and oversight to achieve and maintain the financial and market viability of their organization should be the sole job of a director – whether the organization is a school district, a cooperative, or a pizza parlor.

A good working relationship between the board of directors and the organization's employees is vital to an organization's effectiveness, and this relationship will be different for every organization. Board members for newer, small organizations will often handle some day-to-day responsibilities normally performed by employees in a more mature organization. Even organizations aligned at similar points in their growth cycles will have different needs depending on their circumstances and available resources. Although there is no "right" way for the board and employee relationship to be defined, it is imperative the roles in your organization be very clear and universally understood.

In order for this relationship to be successful, both the board of directors and the employees need to follow whatever parameters have been set for their relationship. Typically, the organization's lead executive, the Chief Executive Officer or General Manager, will be the gateway for most board and employee communications. Exceptions exist, particularly in committee work when an employee is assigned to the committee, but these exceptions should be carefully defined. A danger that exists is the possibility for micromanagement or over involvement by members by the board. Also, grievances taken directly to board members from an employee, unless it pertains to the lead executive, should be redirected appropriately in order to maintain the integrity and trust laid out by board and employee policies.

In general, boards set policies for the organization *as a whole*, including the board and employee relationship, but this does not mean the employees are bereft of policy-making authority. For example, the employee leadership should create day-to-day *operational* policies separate from the organizational policies of the board.

Furthermore, some policies are best formed through *collaboration* between the board and employees. The following chart illustrates some of the policies boards and employee may wish to create and adopt separately and collaboratively.

Board-Created Policies	Collaborative Policies	Employee-Created Policies
• Mission Statement • Conflict of Interest Policy signed annually • Code of Conduct • Board attendance and participation policy • Board self-evaluation • Board education • CEO Evaluation	• A strategic plan with measurable objectives • Financial procedures • Investment management • Sexual harassment and non-discrimination • Gift acceptance • Crisis plans • Financial management, including a rolling two or three year plan	• Hiring, supervising, and terminating of employees • Utilization of the organization's resources (human, physical, technological, etc.) • Marketing/publicity • Lobbying and advocacy • Employment terms • Annual budgets

Generally speaking, the better the collaboration between the board and the employee body, the better the organization will perform. Often, though, conflicts will emerge between senior executives and the board. Priorities will differ, and the most frustrating conflicts will usually occur within a board – usually a non-profit – with a director with an agenda that either doesn't support the organization's best interests or pursues something that is self-serving. Dealing with a board member under these circumstances requires an extraordinary level of patience, diplomacy, tact, and persistence. As long as the conflict and head-butting stays on a rational business level and doesn't become personal, it can usually be resolved over time. Once things get personal, or the board splits in its support for the rogue director, it may be time to start looking for another situation. These types of conflicts tend to be less common within for-profit boards where the CEO may also be the President, Board Chair, and/or a large shareholder.

KEY THOUGHT

Reporting to a Board of Directors can be very rewarding yet very challenging, demanding, and time-consuming. A key challenge for non-profit boards will always be to keep the board focused on improving the business and not catering to their constituency at the expense of the organization's welfare.

Chapter 15:
Personal Development

To prepare yourself for future positions with increasing responsibility, you will want to continue your own personal development. This might be more education – I went back for an MBA – or some other path to help you a) master the current job, and/or b) prepare you for additional responsibility down the road. There are many ways to do this. To name a few:

Education. You can approach this from several perspectives. You can go "deep," or you can go "wide." In other words, you can get a higher level degree in an area you already know, such as getting an MBA on top of an undergraduate degree in some business specialty area. This is a particularly good option if you are in finance or accounting. Going wide means that you broaden your academic credentials in new areas – the classic example being the electrical engineer, with a BSEE or even an MSEE, who goes after an MBA to learn about things financial that become increasingly important as you move up the organizational ladder.

Certifications. Closely related to educational development is earning a professional business certification and credential such as a CPA, CIA, MPM, or the like. Obtaining these credentials will be interesting, rewarding, and challenging to pursue, will increase your contacts within your industry, and will differentiate you from your peers in a very positive, constructive way. Certifications are available in virtually *every* work discipline and can add significant value to an employee's contribution. Some years back I earned a professional coaching certificate from the Institute of Professional Excellence in Coaching (IPEC). I did not intend to become a coach but rather used the knowledge I gained in day-to-day conversations and discussions with employees, professionals, and vendors. It gave me a distinct advantage in establishing and maintaining a good open line of communication with no wrinkles. It helped with counseling and other conversations of a personal nature. I also encouraged our technical people to get as many technical certifications as possible from our vendors and other industry leaders such as from Microsoft, Cisco, Oracle, and so forth. These technical certifications gave these employees a boost in their performance which led to raises and promotions.

Peer Groups. Vistage International is an organization dedicated to improving leadership and management. They function by forming "peer groups" of approximately 12-16 managers at various levels with specific targets. The "CE" groups are for Chief Executives or those holding similar responsibilities with perhaps different titles, e.g., general manager, regional president, vice president, general manager, and so forth.

"Key" groups are just that – key executives who want to sharpen their skills and prepare themselves for greater responsibility at some point. Then there are also specialty groups focused on human resources, accounting and finance, and so forth.

The groups are led by successful leaders from industry, education, and government who act as facilitators and mentors for their group. Typically, a group will meet monthly for a full day with a speaker in the morning with private roundtable discussion regarding various personal issues of concern from the group members in the afternoon. Often, group members will meet each other for lunch or drinks apart from the group to discuss issues of particular concern with another member who has dealt with a similar situation.

It is not uncommon for a good Vistage "chair" to have several groups depending on their time and availability[16]. Vistage is not free, so company or personal sponsorship will be required to participate. The value is there – I was a member of a Vistage CE group for over 10 years and received immeasurable value from the input from my peers in other companies – even in other industries. This is a great developmental option if you can make it work[17]. Get more information on Vistage at www.vistage.com.

Local Boards. Being a board member is usually a form of community service, e.g., being on the board of a non-profit organization or some other service organization in your community. The reality is that you gain good experience learning how boards operate, making good contacts outside your organization, and doing some good for your community. The nice thing about these boards is that they are available to younger people so you could take advantage of this option early in your career. Examples of these types of boards are the Better Business Bureau, Chambers of Commerce, United Way, school boards, government groups like the Workforce Solutions, and many, many others. I have already mentioned my board experiences and the many benefits I received from them.

Industry Associations. These organizations are a great way to learn more about your current industry and make contacts that you can reach out to with various issues and concerns you may have in your organization. Having people to talk to outside your organization becomes invaluable as your leadership career progresses for primarily two reasons – one, they are safe – you can say things to them in confidence that you would not say to someone in your own organization. Second, the response you get will likely not be what you would hear from within your own organization. In fact, you can't find a better place to learn industry best practices than through a good industry association. You can also learn about position openings in other, similar companies if you are willing to make a career move or perhaps relocate to obtain a more responsible position. Board member opportunities with industry associations are *particularly valuable* for networking and learning more about your industry, your peers, and best practices within your industry.

Networking. When networking is mentioned, most people think of cocktail parties with a drink in one hand and business cards in the other. I have been to networking events where the hosts actually offered a prize for the most number of business cards collected during the event. This may be the makings of a great cocktail party, but it isn't going to build your career very much. A true networking conversation is one in which you meet someone with whom you would like to have a business colleague relationship and then create a compelling reason for that person to view you in the same manner. Some basic rules of effective networking are:

- Never ask the prospective colleague for a job; don't ask if the prospective colleague "knows who is hiring" – instead ask if they know if there is a company that has any open roles. People know you are attending a networking event to make contacts for potential career moves – just sound confident, professional, and selective.
- Ask the prospective colleague for advice, information, or referrals, i.e., other beneficial connections that could be made. Most people like to be asked for advice or information, and referrals and connections will come after rapport has been established.
- Then offer some service or favor to the prospective colleague. It doesn't matter what the service might be – in fact they could be very simple – it just needs to be offered. The point is to start off giving instead of taking.

Follow these guidelines at your next networking event and see the difference in the outcome. There is a saying, "great organizations get outside" (or GOGO), and good leaders learn to observe a situation objectively, then execute and gain benefit from it. If you come away with one or two new relationships with enough rapport for follow up discussions, you will have had a successful networking event.

Create a "heroes journey." Write your life story and thoughtfully review the decisions you made at critical points in your past. Review with your *current level of experience* what you might have done differently in the past or how you might have pursued an alternative direction. Reflect *and learn* from your experiences what you might have done better with less emotion and more experience. I have done this, and it is interesting to see how you review and rethink key decisions in your past. An important component of this process is the intellectual honesty that was discussed earlier.

Start Making Reading a Priority. There is an unlimited amount of useful information in business magazines and books, and successful leaders become avid readers and life-long learners. Make time each day to read business blogs or some other business literature. Biographies of successful corporate business leaders, e.g., Jack Welch from General Electric (GE), or Harold Geneen from International Telephone & Telegraph (IT&T) have numerous lessons and tips on surviving in larger organizations. Other books focus on smaller and start-up companies, e.g. Facebook, Google, and SpaceX/Tesla, and have great advice as well. A great quote from Andrew Carnegie (1839-1919), a Scottish-American industrialist, philanthropist, and pioneer in establishing libraries in the United States, makes my point:

"I choose free libraries as the best agencies for improving the masses of the people, because they give nothing for nothing. They only help those who help themselves. They never pauperize. They reach the aspiring and open to these chief treasures of the world – those stored up in books. A taste for reading drives out lower tastes."

It is quite true that *"readers are leaders."*

Part II:
Managing Capital and Strategic Planning

Chapter 16
Key Ingredients

Managing capital and making financial decisions starts with a thorough understanding of your company's profit model and working to improve it by means of a Strategic Plan (the "Plan"). What this means is you have to understand how your organization makes money and how to grow and improve the organization's performance for the benefit of its owners. Before dealing with the actual components of a Plan, take the time to review the purpose of this type of plan and its steps.

Some good resource books to read and review prior to beginning the strategic planning process are:

- *Strategic Planning: A Pragmatic Guide*, by John H. Hobbs and John F. Hobbs
- *Strategic Planning: An Interactive Process for Leaders*, by Dan R. Ebener
- *Strategic Planning Kit for Dummies*, by Erica Olsen
- *Strategic Planning for Non-Profit Organizations*, by Michael Allison
- *Team-Based Strategic Planning: A Complete Guide to Structuring, Facilitating, and Implementing the Process*, by C. Davis Fogg
- *Start With the Vision*, by Robert R. Shallenberger

Also, for your financial analysis development, these books will be helpful:

- *Financial Statement Analysis*, by Martin S. Fridson and Fernando Alvarez
- *Financial Reporting and Analysis*, by Lawrence Revsine, Daniel Collins, et al.
- *Financial Analysis: Fourth Edition*, by Steven M. Bragg
- *The Essentials of Financial Analysis*, by Samuel Weaver
- *Ratio Analy Fundamentals; How 17 Financial Ratios Can Allow You to Analyze Any Business on the Planet*, by Axel Tracy

All of these titles are available anywhere business books are sold.

Chapter 17:
Developing a Strategic Plan

Developing and successfully implementing a Strategic Plan makes two statements about the organization's leadership:

> 1. The organization is serious about their desire to grow, obtain additional market share, and become a dominant player in their market space.

> 2. The organization is serious about improving their profitability through additional market share and better cost control through innovation and economy of scale benefits.

KEY THOUGHT

If the organization does not wish to grow, gain market share, and become more cost effective, there really isn't much reason to go to the time, trouble and expense of creating and implementing a Strategic Plan.

I have seen many, many companies invest in a Strategic Plan just because they thought they had to have one in case anyone asked – but the plan remained on the shelf and gathered dust while they continued to operate as they did previously.

The best method to develop a successful Strategic Plan is for senior management to appoint an interdepartmental team of various levels of successful managers and long-term employees. Generally the senior marketing executives chair the process because of their more extensive knowledge of the external marketplace in general; however, that is certainly not the only committee model that works. The team members will also need to be well-versed in the products and/or services the organization provides and how the market demand might evolve and shift over the next 5-10 years. They will need to be able to forecast an evolution in customer wants and needs and have some idea how to evolve the current product and/or service line to remain relevant in the marketplace. The team members will also need to understand the cost basis of the organization's products and/or services in detail along with innovations to reduce cost/unit sold and grow the customer base with a disproportionately lower increase in costs.

The end game is to profitably grow the organization and achieve greater market share in the process to become a more dominant player in their marketplace.

To get started with a Strategic Plan, the planning team can make the following assumptions:

1. There are more revenue opportunities for the organization than the organization has the time and resources to obtain. Therefore, executives will need to intelligently prioritize their time and resource allocation and its utilization.

2. If an organization is going to explore business growth development, the planning committee will need to thoroughly understand their organization's core business issues and needs in terms of the current industry issues, concerns, problems, and potential solutions and *NOT* just in terms of their company's current products, services, hardware, and/or software.

3. The Plan must be "scalable." That is, it must be able to address corporate, departmental, divisional, or product line level focus – whatever "business entity" in which the organization is a stakeholder. Some plans may be corporate-wide, others will be lesser in scope. They are all important.

4. The best opportunities for organizations to show quicker growth and/or profit improvement in a Plan are typically going to be either with a "winning" business entity or a "losing" business entity of an organization's operation. A "business entity" is defined by the organization, of course; however, what is referred to could be a subsidiary, an affiliate, a product or service line, or a particular functional department of a company. Therefore, the planning team would go through a sorting process to identify the "winners" and "losers" within their organization, simply because when picking initial groups to develop, it is logical and easier to start at the extremes with either winners or losers. More detailed information on identifying and selecting winner and loser entities will come later.

In strategic planning, it is important to be realist and thoughtfully determine whether or not the opportunities uncovered are reasonable. It's admirable to want to grow or diversify to be the next Fortune 500 organization, but there are many steps along the way. Many plans fail because the consequences of *executing* their plan are nct fully considered and vetted. In other words, just because your organization *can* do something doesn't necessarily mean it *should*.

The plan needs to fit the organization's culture and capabilities. Our broadband business had *many* opportunities to overbuild small towns in South Texas – in fact we could have overbuilt as many towns as we wanted to serve. When we looked at the details of what it would take to accomplish these projects, however, we realized we were looking at a 20+ year initiative and not something achievable within a 3-5 year planning scope. We simply didn't have enough staff to competently oversee the number of projects it would have taken, and to execute the original strategic plan would have diverted most of our human and material resources to these growth projects at the expense of satisfying our current customer base. The initial strategic plan was simply far more aggressive than we could have managed and successfully completed. We did, however, scale the plan back and successfully *quadruple* our customer base over a five year period – and that was still very challenging.

Finally, the Strategic Plan should have a section on force and succession planning, i.e., the employees and their leadership. Organizations tend to overlook or willingly ignore succession planning and leadership development which will create voids and slowdowns while vacated leadership positions are open for several weeks or months prior to being filled. Successful organizations expect force turnover and have a bench of trained and developed talent ready to fill open jobs.

One important reason to have good force planning is for acquisitions and new office locations. When an organization is acquired, it is a good idea to have someone from the acquiring organization with strong leadership skills and track record relocate and occupy a key leadership position in the new organization. This is vital to ensure that:

- The acquiring company's culture is instilled into the acquired organization and that there is no dissonance that develops between the organizations with an "us vs. them" mentality.
- The acquiring organization's operational nuances become embedded in the acquired organization's operations, i.e. the acquired organization does business like the acquiring company given the businesses are the same. This facilitates the migration to new IT systems, equipment, vehicles, buildings, and more.
- The acquired organization's products, services, advertising, promotions, sales scripts, and the like become compatible with those of the acquiring organization.

When we overbuilt eleven new towns in South Texas with fiberoptic service, we established an office in a small town not near any of our existing locations. We sent a strong, successful, manager to run that office to be sure the office would be run in a manner that mirrored our home office and other branch locations.   Later, when we acquired a company in a small town east of San Antonio, we moved this strong leader again to ensure the newly acquired business operated according to our standards and guidelines. It was wise to do this as most of the leadership in that office left for one reason or another – most by our choice.

The bottom line is you will have to know who your "disciples" are because you will need them with any growth your organization may achieve.

There are many ways to approach force and succession planning:

- Managers at all levels of leadership should meet formally at least a couple of times per year to review their employee's assessments of potential.   Employees can be rated as "not ready," "ready now," "ready in six months," "ready in one year," etc.   Career pathing for promising future leaders can be as specific as the needs of the individual employee. Some employees may need more formal education, e.g., college, while others would benefit from experience in other work areas to gain other skills.   The time to educate and train future leaders is *before* they are moved up the organization – not *after* when they are struggling to keep up.

- Employees with more than one level of advancement potential should be identified as "high potential" and career-pathed more aggressively than others. High potential employees will typically leave the organization if they do not get the challenges that they need for their job satisfaction.
- Develop and implement a culture of rotating supervisors and managers in different positions to broaden their experience and competence. When employees are rotated through different jobs at their current level of supervision, they see a bigger picture of the organization and gain confidence in their abilities to contribute.

Also, force planning and succession planning should anticipate a need for skills that may be needed in the future that are not necessarily needed now. A good example of this that I recall was when the senior management within the broadband industry did not see a need to train technicians on using computers because the technicians worked with their hands and filled out paper forms as their jobs were completed. As more and more computerized systems came into the marketplace, it soon became obvious that very soon *everyone* in the organization would have to have computer skills and not just in certain positions. I saw a lot of wasted time while organizations took over a year to bring their technicians up to speed on using laptops and smartphone apps for job completion, time and expense reporting, and so forth. If they had just paid attention, they would have seen this evolution as inevitable and better planned for it.

Force planning and succession planning are far more important than most organizations realize. Do not ignore or minimize this important task. It is not difficult, but it does take time and extensive thought.

Chapter 18:
Data Collection for Strategic Planning

In formulating any strategic initiatives, the first thing the committee members must do is to be sure they completely understand the business issues that are important to their organization - first *as a whole business entity* and then *by operating business entities, e.g., affiliates, departments, or divisions* – however they are designated. This means planning committee members must invest time in researching, then learning and understanding the basics of the organization's market place, their industry segment, and the various business models that are in operation in the marketplace.

In today's world, with the internet, resources are plentiful to learn about new businesses. A few research ideas to get started are:

- Google your organization and see what all pops up – market share, litigation, regulatory issues, financial problems, etc. Also check the Google ratings on your organization and see how that compares with the Google ratings of your competitors.
- Look up the web sites for appropriate and relevant industry associations. Look for names of possible additional competitors to your company and be prepared to compare and contrast with your organization. Look up industry leaders and follow their progress and learn from it.

- Review your competitors' web sites and learn where their offices are located, what types of products and services they offer, and where they choose to do business. Make a note of key executives and associations to which they belong.
- Review your competitors' Facebook™, Instagram™, and LinkedIn™ pages. Make notes of awards, recognition, customer comments – both favorable and unfavorable.
- Look up your competitors' key executives on LinkedIn™. What connections are noticeable – schools, former employers? Where do their key people come from? What are their backgrounds, skills, achievement, and awards.

KEY THOUGHT

Not all of the discovered industry issues will be important to each operating business entity; however, a C-Level executive[18] must determine which industry issues are important to a particular business entity and to what degree the issue is important (prioritize the issues as to their importance).

After determining which issues are important to the business entity and the extent to which these issues are important, an executive has completed the first step toward developing a meaningful and professional Strategic Plan.

The next step is to examine and validate these issues in detail by means of organizational interviews and meetings, along with a thorough reading of industry data and discussions with industry leaders and other company executives with similar or greater experience. The identification of possible growth and profit improvement strategies will enable an executive to begin formulating and testing (through actual verification) a Plan to address any potential issues of concern with solutions developed

Obtaining complete financial data provides the planners with an organized source of reliable points of information. An adequate assembly of such data will enhance the quality of judgments made throughout the entire planning process. Data collection should include information on:

- The organization's competition for comparison purposes;
- The organization's marketplace, i.e., their target customer market;
- Present customer operations information;
- How profits are generated and recorded;
- Pertinent financial and operating ratios (key performance ratios – KPIs) and their trends
- Trends and forecasts regarding effects on the organization's operations of external economic and market conditions; and
- The organizational goals, strategies, and overall corporate direction.

Basically, you are researching your *and other* similar companies operating in your current market space.

From the analysis of the information which was gathered, an executive should now be able to draw some conclusions on the business entity's strategy and make some specific assumptions concerning the business entity's abilities to achieve those strategies.

General statements such as "increase profits" should be assumed rather than included or should be broken down into specific numerical goals, timeframes, and specific activities that will impact a Plan.

The organization's goals and objectives which are more easily attainable from external sources will have to undergo further distillation and reduction to the goals, objectives, and "subgoals" of each business entity if applicable. External information and perhaps personal interviews to verify and define some corporate data may be necessary to get a clearer picture of how it relates to various entities within the total organization.

Below is a brief review which will tie these items back to the objectives and purposes of a profit improvement plan:

A business entity profile should include such things as:

- Sizing characteristics
- Revenue characteristics
- Potential – ultimate salable revenue and ultimate obtainable revenue

- Revenue analysis of current company expenditures with the company, i.e., account expenditures with the company as of the current date
- Growth plan, i.e., how does an executive plan to grow the current organizational billings with the current lineup of products and/or services
- Long-term communications plans – internal and external
- Financial data:
    - Income statement (P&L) (by operating business entity if available)
    - Balance sheet (by operating business entity if available)
    - Current Return On Investment (ROI)
    - Desired ROI
    - Desired internal rate of return (hurdle rate)
    - Trend analysis of financial data – five-to-ten-year period if available
- Organizational profile:
    - Actual organization structure
    - Power structure (decision makers, influencers, recommenders)
    - Where do expense dollars go?
    - Growth plans? (past and future)
    - Customer needs (perceived and underlying)
    - Definition of company's marketplace

- Stated objectives
- People profile – an executive should have a profile on every person who has significant input in the decision-making process. This could include personal and professional data.
  - Management style
  - Likes and dislikes
  - Motivations – business oriented
  - Strengths and weaknesses in the management style
  - Perceptions of the organization (positive or negative)
  - Personal and business objectives
  - Business background, e.g., sales, finance, accounting, operations, engineering, etc.

Some useful information sources are listed below and are not ranked by importance, amount of information, or worth. Corporate leaders should examine as many of these sources as possible prior to making any assumptions as to what will be of most value. Note that most of these sources are now available online and may have subscription fees to obtain the level of detail desired. Corporate leaders can pool subscriptions at company level or otherwise share expenses as is reasonably achievable.

Industry Associations

Associations are extremely useful as they provide an overview of the industry in question, major processes, operational issues, advocacy issues, projections, assumptions, and often key metrics used within the industry. Associations often feature "sub-industry segment" information that could be regional, vertical (integrated), or horizontal differences among the many varied companies within the overall industry. Google search the industry and get started.

Industry associations are also good resources to learn how to cope with emergencies and crisis management. Look to the prominent companies to learn how the pros prepare for and navigate tough and challenging times.

Industry Conferences and Seminars

Many industry associations have conferences and training seminars which are invaluable to attend not only for the educational benefit but also making contacts within the industry. It is very handy to have a "go to" person (who is not a company) that can help and coach while an executive comes up to speed on exactly how the industry works. Corporate leaders can also pick up on industry jargon, dress, and customs at industry seminars that will be invaluable at making positive impressions when back at the organization's headquarters location(s).

Trade Journals

Trade publications are plentiful and have much useful information to help in comparisons between your organization and others in the same market space. *Most of these journals and sources below are online these days and are available to non-industry interested parties.*

Standard & Poors

An annual volume, now available online with a companion monthly update, provides an excellent profile on most public companies. Other S&P publications which may be helpful include N.Y.S.E. Stock Reports, Industry Surveys, and The Weekly Industry Outlook. Again, most of these are available online.

Advertising (Key Indicators)

A company's print and electronic media advertising can give insight into what the company is trying to do, how it wishes to be perceived by the public, and in what marketplace it considers itself to be operating. It tells how an organization is attempting to position itself in a specific part of the business and often gives insight into what it feels are the important differentials between its products and/ or services and those of its competitors.

Advertising, more than any other source, can indicate the direction of an organization's marketing strategy. Through an accumulation of advertising over a period of time, a thoughtful executive can determine how the strategies of the organization's business – as well as the overall industry – should change and become more adept at recognizing these changes in the future.

10K Report

This is an annual business and financial report filed by most public corporations with the Securities and Exchange Commission (SEC). It contains two parts; Part I is the financial section filed within 90 days of the fiscal year end. Part II contains the information normally required in a proxy statement. The value of this report is that it provides a common denominator for comparing financial data between companies operating in the same industry. Also consider using 8K, 12K, and 10Q Reports.

These reports can be found online through the SEC's website (www.sec.gov) and generally through the public company's website.

Internal company Publications (Key Indicator)

These include management information bulletins, newspapers, employee magazines, etc. The purpose of these publications is usually to communicate with employees in an effort to keep them informed an organization's activities and direction.

Internal publications are good indicators of new or renewed emphasis by the company or power struggles within the organization. Reading "between the lines" will help with understanding more about an organization's internal affairs. Information about the people who could be a key to an executive's efforts may also be gathered in this manner.

DUNS Review

Each December, Duns ratios for manufacturers are published. These can be used for ratio comparisons between the organization and others in the industry to identify opportunities for growth and profit improvement.

Regulatory Agency Reports

The organization may be required to file operations or financial reports or disclosures to a governmental agency, e.g., Civil Aeronautics Board, Federal Communications Commission, etc. These can often be sources of useful operating data.

Chapter 19

Analyzing Data in Larger Organizations

The numbers from the financial data sources will provide a synopsis of the financial health of your organization and that of your competitors. Most of the sources required are readily available to establish either actual or well-estimated figures for these data. Make your comparisons with industry averages in any one year and detect trends by plotting the figures for three or more years. A simple Excel spreadsheet can do this easily and quickly.

The comparisons made for the organization are the beginning, and similar comparisons will need to be made for each business entity, if appropriate, with their industry averages, their specific competitors and with other operating entities within the company account. Data will be necessary to make comparisons for each market, division, product line, or subsidiary within the company.

Bear in mind that comparisons can be made several ways – prior vs. current performance, trends by different divisions with the account organization, trends compared with industry averages or with specific competitors. These pages suggest some aspects to examine at the outset.

When comparing your organization's performance figures and ratios to detect opportunities for growth and profit improvement, you can make comparisons several ways:

- Compare the business entity with its own past performance;
- Compare it with other operating entities in the same corporate environment;
- Compare it with others in the industry (competitors);
- Compare trends – three years or more;
- Compare against established goals for those periods for the organization or business entity;
- Compare with the economy in general;
- Compare performance before and after major new investments.

You can also follow this process to assess your competitors as well.

It is not necessary when comparing operational statistics of a business entity to be exact in the numbers that are used. The relative size and trends are the important consideration in selecting winners and losers. Without precise quantitative data, estimates can be made on the relative magnitude of contribution or allocation for each division.

Demographics for Review and Consideration

Major Operating Locations: The number of locations where a large workforce is concentrated, or a major process is accomplished.

Minor Operating Locations: The number of locations where medium to small operations are accomplished.

Employees: Total number of employees per division or location.

Major Competitors: The number of competitors which have a large share of the market.

Market Share/Position: How dominant is the organization in its market space? Is the market share large enough to influence pricing, technology, and/or direction?

Revenue

Cash Flow: Where do the organization's revenues come from? Cash will come from operations (sales), investments (interest), or finance (sale of assets). A healthy organization will receive most of its cash flow from operations. Sale of assets will cause a bump in revenues that may not accurately reflect the financial health of the organization.

% Sales: Revenue generated per business entity of total corporate sales. What has been the contribution to corporate revenue from each subsidiary, division, department, region, product line, function, etc. for the last 3-5 years? What do trend lines show comparing rates of growth? Do they meet expectations?

% Net Income: Per business entity of total corporate net income.

Net Income/Sales: Usually listed in financial digests as a separate item, it can easily be computed as:

$$\frac{\text{Net Income}}{\text{Net Sales}} = \text{\% Net Income to Sales}$$

Compared with the industry norm, what picture does this create? If the business entity's net income ratio is lower than those of other operating entities or its external competitors, there may be opportunities to contribute to an improved ratio through reduced cost of sales, reduced overheads, increased sales at a rate faster than costs increase, etc.

This ratio is usually examined in conjunction with the value of sales, the total capital employed, and the turnover or inventory and receivables. For example, a low rate of return of sales compared with a rapid turnover and large sales volume may be yielding earnings quite satisfactory to the account. Make comparisons here between divisions and operating entities as well for a clearer picture of each business entity's relative performance.

% Market Share: This may have already been expressed as an explicit percentage of market in your source area. If not, make a judgement from analysis of the sales dollars of major competitors. Add the sales of the product or service being examined made by all of the companies in the field. Divide the customer's sales of the product by the total to determine the % share of the market enjoyed by the organization.

Has market share and the business entity increased or decreased when compared with competitor's shares over the last 3-4-5 years?

Assets

% **Capital Invested:** Which business entity is obtaining large amounts of investment capital? What has been the pattern for new capital allocation and spending in past years for each operating business entity being examined. Look for deviation from the general pattern.

Look for investments disproportionate to revenue generated and ROI when compared with other entities. How long has the disproportionate capital spending continued in relation to the time "allowed" by company practice for payback (hurdle rate)? Is time running out?

Return on Investment (ROI): The return-on-investment computation relates the major operating and financial factors involved in making a profit to the period of use of the invested funds. The chart on the following page is a graphic representation of how ROI is derived. How does ROI compare to similar organizations within the industry and with other company entities? An ROI that compares poorly with competitors suggests an examination in greater depth to determine the difference and then the application of imaginative and corrective changes in the account systems. Six of the most common variables most commonly affecting ROI are:

Working Assets:
- Inventories
- Receivables
- Cash

Total Expense
- Cost of Sales
- Selling Expense
- Administrative Expense (G&A)

Determine, if possible, what the overall organizational yardsticks are for success. Determine what they are for each operating business entity. What functions are automated – partially? Fully? Where are communications intensive activities? Where are operations still conducted with manual or partially automated processes?

Examine the profit picture for each of the business entities reviewed under revenue generation. Consider that ROI below the industry norm, or less than past performance, may signal an opportunity for a growth or profit-improvement proposal. An ROI that is close to, or less than, the interest rate on high grade bonds or prime interest rate, is rarely going to be acceptable to executive management. The lower the investment risk, usually, the lower the rate of interest or return.

What is the implication of the present ROI in light of product, service, or venture history? ROI should be greater for efforts that required long-term investment to develop and market.

How much technical know-how was involved? Are there patents or exclusive processes involved. ROI should be relatively higher on these. Compare ROIs with the organization's minimal requirements (hurdle rate) as well as with other business entities or other product or service lines in which the organization is invested.

Inventory Turnover: Expressed as "times per year" or "turns," determine inventory turnover by adding the monthly inventory balance on hand and dividing it into 12 (months). Four months' supply, for example, would represent three turns. Another method of comparing inventory turnover among divisions would be to express the end-of-year inventory as a percentage of annual sales for each operating business entity.

Compare inventory turnover with others in the industry in terms of average number of turns per year.

An unfavorable turnover comparison with others in the industry may suggest a communications, mechanization, or automation deficiency in the account's distribution and thereby reduce the working assets required to service a larger volume of sales.

Receivables to Sales: Receivables are viewed in terms of the average collection periods:

Account Receivable = Average Collection Period (Days)
Daily (credit) Sales

Daily (credit) Sales = Net Sales for the Year ÷ 365 days.

Or, simply take the end of the year receivables and express them as a percentage of annual sales.

How does this figure compare with others in the industry or with other business entities or divisions? What is the average time for collection of receivables? How long is the turnover cycle from cash through inventory to receivables? An organization should be compensated for extending credit, so do receivables have discounts for early payment and penalties for late payments?

Expenses

% Administrative Expense (G&A): Concentration of the support required per division expressed as a percentage of the business entity's total sales or operating expense.

The administrative expense is one which most companies do not want to grow faster than sales or other expenses. It is also an area where technology in some manner or format can be a primary vehicle to control expenses. Compare the administrative expense with either sales or total expense or both. Determine a year-to-year comparison to see if it is growing at a faster rate than sales or total expense.

% Data Processing/Information Technology (DP/IT) Expense: Concentration of DP/IT required per business entity expressed as a percentage of the division's total sales or operating expense.

If this data is available on an operating business entity basis, the opportunity comparison will be very valuable. DP/IT expense should be compared in the same way as administrative expense, looking for trends compared to total sales or that operating expense.

Is the DP/IT concentrated in one location or are server and other processing entities distributed over large geographic and cloud areas? What is the dependence of each division on DP/IT for its operations? How does each business entity's use compare with industry norms?

% Social Media & Web Site Expense: Concentration of total social media and web site expense per business entity expressed as a percentage of the business entity's total sales or operating expense.

This information is valuable if available on an operating business entity basis and should be compared in the same way as administrative expenses, looking for trends compared to total sales or operating expense.

For each of the functions listed make a quick judgement on how extensive they are today in their use of technology. The use of a rank order system or weighing scale such as A=High Utilization, B=Some Utilization, and C=Low Utilization, is probably the easiest method of recording this information. This judgement will be based on knowledge of the account, knowledge of other customers, and other inputs from available industry information.

137

How does the social media and web site expense of each operating business entity compare with the industry norm, other internal operating entities, their major competitors, other companies of similar geographical dispersion? What is their dependence upon other types of social media and web sites? Does social media and web site expense as a percentage of other expenses grow at the annual growth rate?   If not, these costs are likely being displaced elsewhere.

Growth Probability

R&D Allocations: Examine past history and current allocations for R&D efforts for signs of special attention and investment in each business entity, subsidiary, or product/service line. Significant changes in patterns here may reveal intentions and activity where technological contributions can develop during the planning period.

% New Capital Allocations: Of particular interest will be the percentage of new capital allocated to each operating business entity, subsidiary, product/service lines, geographical district, or business function. Knowing where the organization is choosing to invest its capital will help in assigning your priorities to operating entities with higher potential.

% Advertising Allocations: Look at advertising allocations as a percentage of sales dollars and treat them as an indication of added attention to a particular operating business entity of the business when you see extraordinary appropriations. Changes in advertising allocations may be indicative of future activity and effort which call for your products and services.

Compare ad dollars with those of competitors and with other product/service lines within the account. Compare advertising allocation (in percent of corporate sales dollars and percent of unit sales dollars). Heavy investment in advertising should yield payback, i.e. sales, over shorter time spans than the capital dollars invested.

Examine ad dollar appropriations in light of product/service maturity or length of time in the market. Are they being spent in the early years of the curve, to extend a peak, or to prop up a decline? What replacement products or services might be in development to replace an ailing product or service being propped up by current advertising dollars?

Determine the growth trends for each operating business entity in each of the indicators developed in this section of the planning process. Three-year charting is usually the minimum to detect a trend – five years is better if it is available.

Summary

At this point an executive should organize available information into three categories – market information, corporate information, and key information by each "division" or operating business entity under study. The information listed by operating business entity will then be used in the next state of planning to select the winners and losers. It will be compared and analyzed in relation to market and corporate information as well as industry norms and competition within the industry.

An example of some of the information you will want to list includes:

- Demographics
  - Major operating locations
  - Minor operating locations
  - Number of employees
  - Major Competitors
- Assets
  - Capital invested
  - Inventory turnover
  - Receivables
- Growth
  - Research and development
  - New capital investment
  - Advertising expense
- Revenues
  - Sales
  - Net Income
  - Market share
- Expenses
  - Administrative
  - Communications
  - Information technologies

The purpose of this stage in planning is to:

- Understand the functions with each of the organization's selected operating entities and how they function;

- Determine the best functional opportunities and test for possible growth and profit improvement initiatives you would include in your Plan.

You will be examining the functions of the organization by weighing various characteristics and using your knowledge to highlight functional opportunities.

The functions of your organization's business and the selected business entities are the major segments of work that together create the business as a whole – production, manufacturing, advertising, legal, marketing, sales, distribution, warehousing, etc. There may be 10 to 20 in any one operating business entity or subsidiary, and similar functions may be called by different names from one business to another. Major functions can also be broken down or segmented into separate functions. From the study and analysis already done to obtain knowledge of the operating business entity, list what should be considered the major functions of the business. The pages in this section identify a few examples. Your list will probably contain 10 to 15 functions.

Analysis in these functions will identify and highlight opportunities to examine. It will help in determining those functions which should be higher or lower on your priority list.

Chapter 20
The SWOT Analysis

At this stage, after the team members have completed their data collection, research, and analysis, it is time to conduct a "SWOT" Analysis. "SWOT" is a time-tested analytical and discovery process for developing strategic plans and stands for Strengths, Weaknesses, Opportunities, and Threats. Strengths and Weaknesses are typically *internally* focused – meaning management has the *control and ability to impact them* and improve them. Opportunities and Threats are then *externally* focused and are *outside the control* of the organization's leadership team.

The time frames for these types of plans will vary greatly depending on the industry segment. A technology company, for example, might not be able to develop a relevant plan for more than 2-4 years because of frequent innovations which can greatly alter the market space and its economics. Other industries not so focused on technology might be able to plan for five, seven, or even 10 years down the road – with assumptions that periodic review will be needed to be sure the plan is still relevant.

Developing the initial SWOT "grid" will be the most difficult part. The planning team members will rarely agree 100% on the organization's relative strengths and weaknesses and the extent to which they are relevant to the organization's success. The same applies to opportunities and threats – the team members will, depending on their knowledge of the overall economic environment and competitor's activities, tend not to agree 100% to the extent to which they are important to the analysis. To add to the difficulty of this process, many times a piece of gathered information can represent *both* an opportunity *and* a threat – this will always bring a discussion to resolve exactly where your organization is positioned. Usually, after multiple sessions of discussion, the team can come to a consensus on all the components and prepare a SWOT grid to share outside the committee. An important part of executing a meaningful SWOT analysis is learning what you know and *learning what you don't know* – then finding out what you don't know.

Once the issues are known and the solutions have been identified/verified, the next step in developing a Plan is developing a series of alternatives along with the quantification of their organizational worth and value from which to discuss and select. This is where the development of a value proposition of each alternative is key to making such an undertaking a success. If a solution only benefits one operating business entity but harms another, it won't move the needle much and will serve no purpose to an executive or the organization as a whole. This means an executive must be able to develop figures which will outline and justify in acceptable detail to the operating business entity the exact dollar amount of cost (expense) that will be reduced or displaced in the business entity's organization by implementation of an executive's Plan recommendation. The executive must also be able to identify how much revenue will be realized with the company's investment (defined as change in revenue for a given change in expense or shown graphically as "$\Delta R/\Delta E$"). In concert with this, the executive will be developing not only company or business entity *revenues* but also company or business entity *expenses* which may be associated with the Plan. In the development of the solutions and the quantification section, other relevant company resources must also be identified and quantified. During this phase of the plan, three types of numbers should be generated:

1. A *per unit* dollar amount of "worth" – or value – to the organization from implementing an executive's profit plan recommendation.

2. A *total* dollar amount of "worth" – or value – to the organization resulting from the recommendation (company worth).

3. "$\Delta R/\Delta E$" relationship which is a dollar amount of expense (or investment) to the organization resulting from the implementation of a recommendation, i.e., the relationship of company worth (R=revenue) and company expense (E=expense of products and/or services to implement) to indicate change in revenue (ΔR) with an associated corresponding change in expense (ΔE).

The overarching concept in this exercise is to achieve an "outsized impact," i.e., an outcome several times – *like 10:1* – benefit with the investment of human and financial capital. This information will enable an executive and other departmental executives to not only prioritize but also to allocate resources throughout the company or operating business entity to achieve the Plan goals.

There are several other components of a good SWOT analysis and discussion which add value to the planning process. For example:

- The current perception of the customer base needs to be studied. How do the organization's customers perceive the value of its products and/or services? Do they view the organization as a valuable provider – maybe even with a business partner relationship?

- What market share does the organization have? It is a big fish in a small pond or a small fish in a big pond? This is very important when planning growth and where your organization will look for new customers and how it will appeal to them to become your customers.

- How does the organization's pricing position them in their marketplace? Are they positioned and perceived as the Cadillac of services with Cadillac value, or are they positioned and perceived as the lowest cost provider and essentially a commodity in their marketplace? How is the organization priced and positioned in comparison with its competitors?

- Is there a need to conduct market research to obtain some of these answers and opinions? Developing a strategic plan is not a good time to guess or make unfounded assumptions.

The discussions held during SWOT development offer an opportunity to discuss some very important topics that will factor into your strategic planning:

- **Identification Of the Desired Marketplace.** Where can you obtain the greatest return for the capital you plan to expend? What geography has the most potential? Do you want to focus on urban and community areas with a denser customer population but more competition or in rural and remote areas that have little or no competition.

- **Customer Base.** What *size* of customer is the organization best equipped to accommodate? Small mom and pop operations? Middle-sized companies or larger, national companies? Is there a "sweet spot" where the organization's offerings resonate better than the competition's? What *vertical markets*, e.g. industries might the organization have more opportunity to differentiate from their competitors and gain market share?

- **Customer Acquisition.** Is the organization's capital better invested in organic growth or by acquisitions of similar organizations? Organic growth is slower but can more easily be assimilated into the culture of the organization. Acquisition growth is usually much quicker[19], but integrating a new employee body into the acquiring organization's culture and operational characteristics might take longer than expected and cancel some of the benefits of gaining the new customer base.

146

* **Customer Retention.** How will the organization prevent poachers from taking customers away? Customers can be very fickle[20] and leave for a few pennies per month in savings – what customer loyalty program might diminish those occurrences?

* **Marketing and Advertising.** How has the organization presented itself in the marketplace to date? Has it been effective? Is an image change appropriate with growth and a larger geographic footprint as the organization moves from a local to a regional marketplace?

* **Building and Protecting a Brand.** Does the organization's products and/or services lend itself to a "brand?" Does it have a trademarked name or logo? Is it suitable for anticipated growth, or does it need a facelift and upgrade?

* **Pricing and Positioning.** Many organizations view pricing as a "cost plus" equation with a cost, margin expectation, then price. Price, however, can also be used to convey an image of the organization's products and services. Mercedes and BMW do not utilize cost plus pricing because the price is, in their world, part of the product. Same thing with Rolex and other fine watches. You can't build a reputation as a high quality product or service unless you have a comparable price. The organization's marketplace will usually reveal what the organization can charge, and if the organization's product or service does not have the value

proposition that Mercedes and BMW have, pricing is going to always be a challenge.

- **Competition.** How does the organization define its competitors? Those that offer the same products or services that it does or those who offer a substitute for the products and services it offers? What this means is that the organization must look beyond the organizations that offer similar services and look at those who can substitute. As an example, Southwest Airlines must look beyond United Airlines and American Airlines as competitors and consider train, bus, and automobile travel – travel times being equal – as potential losses of airline seats. Every car on the highway is a seat that Southwest did not or could not sell. How the organization defines and plans for competitors is extremely important in its scope.

It is important to create the right mindset for this project. Does the organization truly want growth or is it largely focused on self-preservation? What initiatives are the organization willing to take to achieve those objectives? There is an excellent Harvard Business Review article by Theodore (Ted) Levitt called *Marketing Myopia*[21]. In the article, Professor Levitt illustrates with examples how organizations get stagnant and lose their creativity. The first great example is in the 1930s when television was first invented, the movie studios were the natural place to nurture this budding industry. They had the talent under contract, the studio equipment, the financing, the distribution, etc. to build a new revenue stream. Instead the studio executives stated loudly and clearly that "they were in the movie business – not the television business" – and let others create immense wealth from television. When the airlines first began operating, the railroads had terminals, freight business, ticketing systems, customer service employees – all available to annex this new means of crossing the country. But the railroad executives all cried, "we're in the railroad business – not the airline business" – and let others create immense wealth in the airline business. Time would educate the movie people that they were not in the movie business but rather the *entertainment* business – an important distinction. The railroad people also went on to learn that they were in the *transportation* business – not the railroad business. It is important to understand that hundreds of billions of dollars *didn't get made* because these businesses had grown stale and didn't understand what business they were actually in. Even in my former industry, telecommunications, in 1878 Alexander Graham Bell offered to license his patents for the new telephone device to Western Union, which, not realizing both organizations were in the *communications* business, refused the offer out of hand. "Who would want to talk over a wire when you already have a telegram?" The rest is history.

This is all to say that planning your organization's future requires *two* types of thinking:

> 1. The "convergent" thinker who thinks "inside the box." These types of thinkers are important because they are focused on current issue

resolutions and solving today's problems. They are invaluable in keeping the current organization on course and moving forward with today's goals and objectives. They maintain the status quo which is important in the short term.

2. The "divergent" thinker is a disruptor who thinks "out of the box" and is focused on the future. They will come up with a dozen off the wall business ideas and present them. Most will be duds, but one or two will be solid gold. Unfortunately, many companies consider these employees to be dreamers or wackos and, to their detriment, undervalue their contributions and the potential they uncover.

The optimal future of the organization will likely be determined by disruptive *divergent* thinkers rather than the *convergent* thinkers.

Be sure to "Red Team" the plan for flaws.

At this point, the SWOT analysis and strategic plan is complete and should now be tested for reasonability and viability. The planning committee should let other *non-committee members* of various levels within the organization review the SWOT analysis and resulting plan, challenge it, and poke holes in it. This team is called a Red Team, and its goal is to find reasons *not* to pursue the recommendations coming from the SWOT analysis and resulting strategic plan. Red Team members should be the most skeptical "Doubting Thomases" that the committee can find. Once the Red Team has completed its review, the SWOT analysis and strategic plan will either hold together or it will not. If it does, an Execution Plan is the next step. If it does not, the planning committee should regroup and recalculate the discrepancies until the Red Team is comfortable with the plan. The concept of a "post mortem" is commonly understood – the "after action" discussion to assess and learn what went wrong or what could have gone better in a sale, business deal, acquisition, whatever. Think of the Red Team review as a "pre-mortem" where the look deep for problems and resolve them prior to their failure once implemented. You want to get to the root cause of any potential problems or miscalculations with the "five whys" process:

1. *Why* would the market expansion not bring success within the plan's timeline? Because we didn't sell enough.

2. *Why* would we not sell enough? The product was not available in sufficient quantities.

3. *Why* would the product not be available in sufficient quantities? Because the manufacturer did not have sufficient quantities of raw materials.

4. *Why* would the manufacturer not have sufficient quantities of raw materials? Because the manufacturer single-sourced the raw materials with a foreign company that did not deliver.

5. *Why* would the manufacturer single source the raw materials with a foreign company that did not deliver? They took the lowest bid with no back up supplier.

The resolution in this example would be to be sure the supply chain had adequate inputs to ensure a reliable flow of new products when they are most needed on an aggressive launch.

Develop An Execution Plan.

The executive must now develop an execution plan of action to implement what has happened so far. The executive must develop a plan implementation *schedule* during which business problems and issues will be defined and the solutions presented to the company or business entity executives and a favorable "buy in" received. This plan should be subdivided into individual and specific activities and their specific timeframes for completion. Those activities should be laid out by time, in other words, a schedule should be made which tells the order in which the steps will be conducted. After the activities have been subdivided and time-framed into a schedule, responsibilities for implementing those steps must be established. The steps for which an executive will be responsible should be identified and posted with completion dates documented. Steps that support forces (technicians, engineers, software technicians, manufacturing, customer service, trainers, etc.) are to meet should be established with committed completion dates and transmitted to the appropriate levels of supervision in the coordinating departments for inclusion into their respective work assignments.

Chapter 21

Management of Normal Growth

As part of any strategic initiative, it is essential to determine how to continue the normal business as usual (BAU) and revenue growth for the organization. The objective is two-fold – to improve the value of the operating business entity to the organization and to protect the business entity's revenues from the invasion of a competitor.

Tactical Support Plan. A tactical support plan should now be developed and documented outlining support activities and the skill levels required to manage the company or operating business entity's day-to-day activities. Looking at each individual business entity or operating component, an executive must determine the revenue to expense ratios for managing growth. This includes base revenue and growth revenues as projected. The expense refers to the skill levels involved.

There is one key assumption which must be drawn when managing growth – to grow existing market share and not lose business to a competitor. Three major categories should be assembled for this section of the major planning and management process:

Basic Inventory of Raw Materials, Existing Products and Services Used. This list should include an inventory of all the various products, services, and raw materials used by your company that are procured from your vendors. You want to establish a baseline expense for what your organization is spending and look for opportunities to change vendors to achieve the same or better for less cost.

Contract Expirations: Which contracts are up for renewal over the next 12-18 months? This is an opportunity to negotiate incentives for your organization to renew early and achieve more favorable terms – or to change vendors if that is more appropriate.

Existing Systems Nearing Capacity. If your internal systems, ERP[22] for example, have physical or logical limits, e.g., a physical or software upgrade needed to meet future organizational growth, you'll want to investigate upgrading now to be ready for future growth and not slow your growth down waiting on product or service intervals. The goal is to achieve and maintain operating diligence and efficiency.

We did a management study several years ago because our business systems were suffering from integrations that failed on a regular basis. Our customer service and billing systems were separate from but integrated with our mapping system, and a couple of times per month one of the two systems had some software update that broke the integration – so that when a customer service representative tried to find a potential new customer location on our maps, the system would not display the map area but would give a blank screen instead. Our IT technicians would then start contacting both the mapping company and billing company to find out who made changes without telling anyone, and no one ever confessed during the first round of questioning. In our study we learned that we had nine – yes *nine* – disparate systems that had been implemented over the years all trying to communicate with each other. We were growing rapidly at the time, and this collage of dysfunctional systems was holding us back. We then decided to throw everything out and replace all nine systems with a single, integrated system with a single data base. Every employee that used any one of the previous nine systems had to be retrained and get comfortable with the new system, but we had no choice. Like all major change, it was rough in the initial weeks, but over time, our operations smoothed out, and people were saying "we should have done this sooner." It was extremely disruptive, but we could not have grown to the size we reached without this part of our management of our growth.

Sometimes you have to throw out the "good" to achieve the "better." We had millions of dollars in Siemens switching equipment that was outdated and was replaced by Metaswitch "soft switch" technology that took up about a tenth of the space of the old Siemens switch and used about a tenth of the power to run it. It was hard to let go of the old equipment, and there was resistance to change. We had technicians that were in their early 50s that knew the legacy Siemens technology like the back of their hand. Overnight their knowledge and troubleshooting experience became irrelevant and useless. On cutover morning, the only comment the switching supervisor had was that he thought the cooling fans on the new equipment were too loud. A couple of the technicians transferred, but most of them approached the new technology with curiosity (which all good technicians have) and started to learn the new technology. They ended up really liking it, and one technician, Wayne T., actually postponed his retirement by over five years because he liked the Metaswitch soft switch technology so well.

Future Plans. Is your organization planning an acquisition? Opening a new office? Expanding an existing office? If so, these are opportunities to negotiate favorable terms prior to your organization's needs.

- A growth plan ensures that your organization is equipped to meet your customer demands. This advanced knowledge can enable your company to be sure there will be no delays or hiccups in meeting your market's current needs.
- A growth plan will also uncover any outlying customer satisfaction issues and get them resolved asap to your company's satisfaction. A potential barrier to expansion can be addressed and resolved before any business is lost.
- A growth plan positions you and your organization for a long-term, profitable, relationship with its customers under any circumstances.

To summarize this point, the Plan should provide a synopsis of current goods and services purchased within your market space – the more granular the information the better. You will need good judgment with this information not to overload the rest of your executive team with too much data but to keep it relevant to their needs. Your plan should quantify and define a normal growth percentage expectation and contemplate how broadening your revenue base by replacing competitor goods and/or services might happen.

Your plan should have a good, detailed analysis of both your direct[23] and indirect[24] competition. Differentiation which could lead to displacement of your competitors should be developed and communicated within your account team to keep everyone focused on broadening your revenue base.

When you plan for revenue growth, be sure to include any increases in expenses that may accompany the revenue increases. This will ensure that the new revenues remain as profitable (or more so) than in previous years. You will also want to be specific in exactly how you will ensure the future growth of your company revenues and specifically how you plan to displace competitive goods and services.

The tactical (action) plan will spell out who is to do what and by what date. These plans should include activities, objectives of those activities, time frames, force requirements, key customer/account contacts, and resources needed to support your efforts from other parts of your company's organization.

Additionally an important part of planning for growth is how to handle emergencies and catastrophic disasters. In our South Texas service area, I have mentioned the frequency of storms which can interrupt operations for some period of time. Our organization developed a disaster recovery plan for major storms which was so good that the Texas Public Utilities Commission used it as a model to send to other broadband companies in Texas. The disaster recovery plan simply anticipated what staff, materials, vehicles, and equipment would be needed at various stages of the disaster so that we could have it in place when needed. We reviewed and updated the plan every June at the beginning of hurricane season. When the wind and rains came, we were ready.

The pandemic was an awful experience, but it was less intrusive because we had already identified which employees could be deployed for remote home operations, and their desk telephones and computers were quickly deployed to their homes as the travel restrictions tightened up. As people became homebound and wanted more broadband service at their homes, we were able to handle a 40% increase in order volume without too much difficulty. The problems we didn't expect – as mentioned earlier – were the technicians being quarantined because people would not tell us they had been exposed to the COVID-19 virus until we were in their home installing or upgrading their service. We did not expect to have so many capable technicians sidelined because they became quarantined[25] as well.

Planning for these types of emergencies should be done formally, thoroughly documented, and available for all employees to access either on paper, a smartphone app, or on a company internal website.

Chapter 22

Opportunity Selection and Evaluation

As an executive leading the organization or division, you need to be constantly evaluating opportunities and anticipating where in the organization's resources should be deployed. The premise here is that good business people need to be constantly evaluating opportunities. They may evaluate at least five or more opportunities at any one given time. Maybe two don't work out because the timing isn't right and are rejected. Two more don't work out because the financing required isn't or won't be available in time. The first four may or may not work out, but the fifth opportunity wouldn't have been evaluated were it not for the other four. The fifth one may also happen in the future, but it would not have been an opportunity had it not be formulated and considered previously. We typically were evaluating *six to ten* opportunities at any given time. Maybe only two or three grew legs, but when they were implemented they were successful because they were thoroughly vetted to be sure they fit with our overall growth strategy, our work force capability, compatibility with our other products and service, and the financial resources necessary to make the opportunity successful.

The planning committee should have a corporate-wide profile prepared for a potential opportunity selection to:

- Get to know the organization's business and direction better;
- Make a better judgment after analyzing all the data on the position of each business entity within the company – the identification of operating business entity's "winners" and "losers";
- Identify product or service lines, divisions, and/or departmental functions that are likely to offer immediate growth and profit improvement opportunities; and
- Develop a concise and relevant input package for the planning process. This package will consist of a brief summary of background information, issues, or questions that should be considered prior to making company presentations.

The method employed in this process is the selection of those entities or products which are "winners" and those that are "losers." *Winners* are those entities that are stronger, usually growing, and highly profitable operations. *Losers* are those that have weaker, typically contracting, and marginal or unprofitable operations. The following are typical characteristics of these two extremes:

Stronger Divisions (Winners)
Highly Profitable Operations
- They typically have higher potential;
- They have more executive visibility, power, and support;
- They attract talent and the best people;

- They are well-funded with both capital and marketing expense;
- They usually are able to take more risks;
- They may be in a growth marketplace with multiple growth opportunities;
- They may already be getting a good ROI with plenty of upside;

Weaker Organizations (Losers)
Marginally Profitable or Unprofitable Operations
- They usually have the greatest opportunity for improvement and greater visibility;
- They may be looking for help to improve their operations or prepare for divestiture, carve out, or sell off;
- They may have key people assigned by the home office;
- They may be at the beginning of a cycle of new funding for profit (new advertising funding and capital investment);
- They will very likely have a lesser degree of effective modernization in their systems or even have passed up on improvements in the past.

The "winners" will typically have more advantages when developing a Strategic Plan. First, they probably already have the highest return on investment which means they will likely have the budget money to pursue opportunities. They probably have a large share of the market in the product or service they take to market and are likely to dominate their segment of their marketplace. They probably have the best people. They probably have a lot of money going into research, new product development and advertising. Their products or services are probably on the growth portion of the product/service life cycle, and they are probably innovative and have budget money to spend.

The other possibility for opportunity is picking a losing business entity or product. The reason for this is that they are probably in trouble and not viewed favorably by senior management. They need help and normally want and are receptive to help. They may even be in trouble because they have not kept up with technology and are operating with dated, high-cost, inefficient systems. In other words, they haven't used modern technology and are behind. You can typically find a lot of things to work on in a losing division or department as well as people that are open to and want help.

There are some precautions in selecting the losing business entity, however. You should first make sure that the company *really wants* to make the losing business entity or product a winner. Before dedicating a lot of time and resources to a losing business entity or product, you should be reasonably certain that the organization is going to allocate the budget money to pursue whatever Plan it is you want to propose to them. You might run into a situation with a loser, that no matter how good your proposal is, the company will not allocate the budget dollars necessary because they're going to sell off or close that division or eliminate that business entity or product.

There are indicators that will tell you if an organization wants to bring a business entity or product from loser to winning category. The first of these is new management. Moving a management team from a winning division to a losing division could be a sign that the organization wants to turn the situation around and has no intention of selling the business entity off. This strategy ties back to an old Wall Street Journal article that Peter Drucker, the well-known business author and guru, wrote called The Five Deadly Business Sins[26]. As he writes, Sin #5 is "feeding problems and starving opportunities" by always assigning the good people to problem solving. When you solve a problem, you get, as Drucker puts it, "damage containment" and nothing more. Only opportunities can bring produce results and bring growth, so smart organizations put their best people on *opportunities* and not *problem-solving*.

Other signs are an increase in advertising – more than their normal proportion or getting more capital resources than in the past. These are all indications that mean the company is willing to invest some capital dollars into converting a loser into a winner.

There are certainly opportunities between these two extremes. Depending on how many entities there are, it often pays to start on the two extremes and work inward toward the other business entity. The number and types selected will vary by organization. Where the majority of the business is in the middle, then naturally a larger amount of work will move toward these entities. Don't exclude a very large portion of the business just to deal with extreme deviations at each end.

One key thing to remember is that all business growth and projects incur some level of risk, and risk makes people nervous. Sometimes risk becomes a negative motivator and stifles plans to grow and expand due to fear of failure. This is understandable but not acceptable.

Another point to remember is that organizations tend to have "lifecycles" just like products. As a reminder, with products, your typically experience:

- **Introduction.** The product is new and unknown. Early adopters jump on, but the market waits to see how the new product performs, how it holds up during use, and how resale values hold.
- **Rapid Growth.** The product now gains "street cred" in the marketplace and takes off. The "wait and see" buyers now enter the marketplace and buy. Market share grows and the product usually becomes profitable.
- **Dominance.** The product reaches its maximum market share and maximum profitability. It is the dominant product of its kind in the marketplace.
- **Decline.** New products now enter the marketplace with more functionality, features, bells and whistles. Purchases of the dominant product now shift to the new entry although the dominant product is still profitable.
- **Death.** The product is no longer relevant or a force in the marketplace. If the organization

does not renovate or rejuvenate the product, it will wallow along indefinitely and hopefully will remain profitable. Once the profitability wanes, the product is removed from the marketplace and goes in the "do you remember when" file.

The classic business school model of this cycle phenomenon can be illustrated with Coca Cola. Coca Cola had achieved dominance in its cola marketplace and competitors like Pepsi Cola and RC Cola were nibbling away at its market share with aggressive advertising and pricing. While Coca Cola had limited growth in the cola marketplace, they had unlimited growth in other sectors. Enter Sprite – now Coca Cola could grow and not cannibalize its cash crop revenue stream in the cola market. There was plenty of growth in the "uncola" marketplace which Coca Cola entered into with a vengeance. Once the "uncola" marketplace reached a saturation, the next open market was Dr Pepper with their very loyal customer base. Enter Mr. Pibb, and Coca Cola grew again. They repeated their strategy with Tab and Diet Coke, etc. and still continue to grow.

Getting back to analysis, pay attention to industry segment life cycles. If you had conducted your study in the early 2000s, Blockbuster would have shown up as a "winner" right before it became a "loser." Netflix and Amazon.com would have shown up as "losers" right before they became "winners." In reviewing and analyzing organizations, it is very important to consider where the organization is within its "lifecycle" segment as this will make a huge difference in your strategies going forward. If the studied organization is in a dying or contracting segment, it is unlikely to present much of an opportunity for immediate growth.

The object of the game is to *anticipate and identify* potential problems by planning, then *mitigate, minimize, or eliminate* those risks with a solid plan. Said another way – if you plan a trip from Houston to Chicago, you can just get in your vehicle and start driving, *or* you can plan your trip.

Your trip plan would contemplate:

- What is the best highway route to take?
  - Do you have a GPS available to assist you if you get lost or if there is a major detour in the planned route?
  - Is an Interstate Highway available or will you have to travel on two-lane roads?
  - Is the trip during a holiday weekend? Will there be heavier than usual traffic?
  - What is the weather forecast for each leg of the trip? Is rain, sleet, or snow in the forecast? Will you remember to take adequate clothing for a change in the weather?
- How many miles you can safely drive in a single day? How many days it will take to make the trip?
  - How much gasoline will be required with the vehicle you will be driving?
    - How much will that cost? Will you have enough cash or credit cards available?
  - How many nights at a hotel or motel you will require during the trip?

- Where will you need to spend the night?
- What hotels are near the highway?
- How much do they cost? Will you have enough cash or credit cards available?
  - How many meals you will need during the trip?
    - What restaurants are near the highway?
    - How much will they cost? Will you have enough cash or credit cards available?

You get the idea. Which trip would you rather experience – the "get in your vehicle and drive" trip or the planned trip shown above? Which trip is likely to have the fewest problems? Which trip is likely to get to the destination on time and on budget?

Mitigating, minimizing, and/or eliminating risk is done through careful, detailed planning – with contingencies built in for expected deviations from what is initially planned. While risk usually cannot be fully eliminated, it can certainly be reduced to a manageable level which does not prevent the success of the initiative or project at hand.

KEY THOUGHT:

You minimize or eliminate risk by careful, thorough planning.

Chapter 23

Management & Strategic Plan Review

In order to review a management and/or a strategic plan prior to submission to your senior management for resource allocation, review your Plan as objectively as possible using these guidelines or checkpoints:

Executive Summary

An Executive Summary should be in the front of each Plan, updated (at least) annually or as needed, to provide your leadership with a ready-made reference tool for decision making on resource and expense allocation.

This is a tool your leadership will use to manage resources and budget dollars, (i.e., staffing, funds, and time) effectively in terms of revenue to expense. Because the Executive Summary is a tool for your leadership, it should provide specific guidelines to fit their management styles. Typically, the summary will address revenue and expense, objectives of the plan, benefits to the account, strategy synopsis, interdepartmental cooperation plan, assumptions, and a validation process.

Business Entity Profile[27]

The Plan should articulate and assess the financial history (usually 3-5 years) of the appropriate operating business entity as well as its projected financial growth. The financial profile should be expressed in terms of an analysis of management philosophy and policy, assets, net worth, sales, major expenditures, cash flow, leverage, ROI, profits, etc., as related to the business sector. Key business financial ratios should be compared with those ratios of others of the same business sector. Information about various operating business entity characteristics will assist you in developing your objectives, strategies, and tactics within the Plan.

Typically, the Plan profile will address:
- The area if business the organization or operating business entity is engaged;
- Management strategic objectives, both short and long range in a narrative format;
- Business concerns, issues, needs, and problems both short and long range. Have they been vetted as a viable opportunity?
- How the organization or operating entity manages its business, both internally and externally, i.e., IT practices (the extent to which technology is used as a management trending tool or as a real-time decision-making tool), marketing and advertising policies, social media status and presence, image relationships with competitors, legal and accounting counsel, benefit programs, etc.

Note: *Assumptions provide the parameters within which decision-making for resource allocations are made. Because the business environment is never static, you must anticipate changes (or the lack of it)* *relative to your organization or operating business entity over time.*

Assumptions should address variables concerning internal and external influences; the sales program (i.e., quality of information in your plan, how long you have represented accounts, etc.) support programs (i.e., experience level of support personnel, turnover rate, etc.), other department real and potential problems (i.e., business office, operations, engineering, administration, etc.) and competition.

Final Thoughts

Putting all these disparate pieces together will take time and a commitment to developing and embracing a long term successful leadership style. Leading with a concern for employees, a focus on their development, a focus on expense management, good planning, and a clear understanding of who you are *and who you aren't* will lead your organization to a favorable end result.

Many times things won't go your way, and you have to go to war and fight Often a competitor will throw a curve that no one was expecting. It was always frustrating to see the larger companies – particularly the cable companies – literally give away service for a year to gain customers at our expense. You then put on the gloves and hit back as best as you can.

Sometimes your business partners do your organization wrong, and you have to take them to court to restore the contractual agreement and its terms. We sued a business partner who we thought was underpaying us, and it took years to resolve the matter. But we felt we had no choice but litigation to resolve the matter. Litigation should be an absolute last resort – always attempt negotiating rather than file a lawsuit. Once the matter is in litigation, you lose all control of the outcome. This is especially true if the matter goes to trial – as you will have no control at all over what happens in a courtroom. It's not going to be about the facts – it's going to be about who tells the best story.

Never forget that business tends to be cyclical, and you will experience good years, not so good years, and really tough years. Remember the 9/1 manager profile and think long and hard about laying off half your work force to improve profits. Yes, it's easy and shows quick results, but the loss of the terminated employee talent along with the loss of the trust, morale, and engagement of the remaining employees will, over time, cancel and undo much of the savings. If you plan to grow, it will be much more difficult if not unachievable. The future of your organization depends on what you chose to do; be careful not to put your organization on a negative trajectory with short term thinking.

The best course of action is usually always to put the welfare of the organization as the top priority and then let nature take its course. If you feel the odds are with you, go for it. If you don't feel good about what to do, the optimal decision is usually not to do it.

Appendix

Financial Analysis and Modeling for Corporate Leaders

The intended outcome of solving any business problem is improved organizational performance. In most instances, organizational performance is assessed through quantitative measures, e.g., return on investment, earnings per share, productivity indexes, lost time due to accidents, and so forth. Because organizational performance is determined through such quantitative measures, analyzing an organization's business problems and issues is a simpler task than you might think. Any quantitative measure involves two factors: 1) the variable or variables that constitute the measure, and 2) the relationships that exist among and between the variables. Although the numeric value of the variables may change, the relationships are constant – indeed, they are literally static. Thus, they can be analyzed independently of the numeric values of the variables. An example will help clarify this point.

One of the most common and most important business measures in use today is Return on Investment (ROI). ROI can be and is calculated in a number of ways; however, one of the more common ways is as follows:

ROI =   Net Profit   (expressed as a percentage)
Owner's Equity

For any given organization, the dollar (numeric) values of Net Profits and Owner's Equity will vary from year to year and, normally, ROI will vary. However - regardless of the numbers involved, when using the ROI formula shown above, ROI is always equal to Net Profits divided by Owner's Equity – that relationship is fixed. To analyze any "ROI" problem, then, you cannot just look at the dollar values of Net Profits and Owner's Equity alone, you must also examine the relationship of those values (in this case it is the ratio of one to the other).

Let's look at another example – Gross Sales. The dollar value of an organization's Gross Sales will vary from year to year (hopefully, it is an upward trend). However – what does that really tell us? Not much for Gross Sales is measured as follows:

Although we know from its numeric value that Gross Sales varies, we don't know why it varies. Is it due to an increased number of units sold? Is it due to an increase in the unit price? Is it due to some combination of the two? Thus, even in a simple measure such as Gross Sales that are a number of variables and certain relationships between them.

Measures of an organization's business performance can become quite complex, involving numerous variables and complex relationships. Regardless of the complexity of the measure, it can be broken down and understood by following a few simple analytical rules. Let's take one more example, and by presenting the analytical rules one at a time, analyze a business problem.

General Rule 1: Find out which measures your company uses to gauge the management and performance of the business.

Measures of business performance abound, and there is not always agreement about how useful or how valid they are. As a result, most businesses tend to decide for themselves which measures are valid and important *to them*. Of course, there are some widely accepted measures such as ROI, earnings per share, and others. In some instances, organizations even construct their own measures that have special significance to their business operations. Adhering to this rule ensures that your analysis of your company's business problems will always begin with those problems that are near and dear to your company's heart. In this way, you will always be attuned to your company's priorities.

In many companies you will find measures on Return on Assets Managed (ROAM). Just as with ROI, there are a number of ways to calculate or compute ROAM. This brings us to the second rule:

General Rule 2: Find out how your company calculates or computes the business measures they use.

This rule is important for two reasons: 1) differences in the way that measures are calculated or computed, and 2) the requirement to identify the variables involved and the relationships among those variables. In this case, ROAM might be calculated as follows:

Earnings (Profits Before Taxes) = Earnings as a % of Net Sales

Net Sales

$$\frac{\text{Net Sales}}{\text{Inventories + Receivables}} = \text{Asset Turnover (\%)}$$

Asset Turnover X Earnings as a % of Net Sales = ROAM

If we were to lay out this calculation in a manner similar to the master economic model shown in Figure 1, we would get a simple "tree chart" like the one shown in Figure 2. Here, we can see the variables and their relationships. ROAM is the product of Asset Turnover and Earnings as a % of Net Sales. Asset Turnover is the quotient of Net Sales divided by the sum of Inventories and Receivables. Earnings as a % of Net Sales is the quotient of Earnings divided by Net Sales. We could continue this breaking down process: Earnings, for example, is the difference between Gross Profits and Expenses – however, we don't need to go that far at this point.

By examining the tree chart of the variables and their relationships, we can begin to see how the relationships affect the variables. We can also see that the _relative rate of change_ in relationships is of extreme importance. If, for instance, Earnings are increasing at a rate faster than Net Sales, Earnings as a % of Net Sales will increase, increasing ROAM. If the sum of Inventories and Receivables is increasing at a rate faster than Net Sales, Asset

Turnover will decrease, decreasing ROAM. In essence, the relationship between the variables will tell you what kinds of changes need to be made in order for a given measure to be affected in the desired direction. As sub-rules under Rule 2, we have:

General Rule 2a: Identify the variables involved in the measure;

General Rule 2b: Identify the relationships between the variables;

General Rule 2c: Identify the kinds of changes that are required to show improvement.

Rule 2c provides a general strategic context for the balance of your analysis. Say for example your company uses ROAM as a key business measure. In order to influence ROAM in a positive direction, you now know that you will have to do one or more of the following:

1. Increase earnings as a % of Net Sales
   a. Cause Earnings to increase at a rate faster than Net Sales
2. Increase Asset Turnover
   a. Cause Net Sales to increase at a rate faster than the sum of Inventories and Receivables, which might be accomplished simply by the levels of Inventories and Receivables.
3. Some Combination of #1 and #2.

However, without specific information about the numeric value of these variables, selecting a precise strategy would be difficult. This brings us to our third and fourth rules:

General Rule 3: Determine the current value of each variable.

General Rule 4: Determine the "standard" for each variable.

Business problems are defined as measurable discrepancies between actual and desired conditions or outcomes. These "gaps" can exist at the financial, operational, and functional levels of an organization. As you can see from the examples so far, problems, or "gaps" can also exist within those three levels. Our "ROAM" problem, for instance, could involve an earnings problem, a sales problem, an inventory problem, or a receivables problem. Thus, for each variable involved in a given business measure, you must identify the desired and actual conditions. This brings us to the fifth rule:

General Rule 5: Identify any discrepancies between actual and desired conditions for each variable involved. In other words, what do you want the outcome to be?

General Rule 5a: If there is a discrepancy, determine whether or not your company considers it important.

General Rule 5b: If your company does not consider the discrepancy important, begin the analysis of another measure.

General Rule 5c: If your company considers the discrepancy important, continue the analysis of the measure.

General Rule 5d: If there is no measure of importance to your company left to analyze, terminate the analysis.

Our last sub-rule brings us to the final rule for analyzing business problems. Assuming you are in pursuit of a discrepancy that is important to your company, the question arises as to when you stop your analysis. In other words, "how long do I keep up the process of analysis?" The answer is in our sixth and final rule:

General Rule 6: Continue analyzing a given business measure for variances until you find a variance which you can impact through an application of some improved process or technology, or until you run out of variables to analyze.

If, for instance, you discovered that inventories and/or receivables were out of tolerance, you might stop your analysis at that point, thinking that those are the two variables that you can directly affect through a process redesign or technology application. This rule recognizes that you are unique individuals; that is, for a given variance, you are likely to come up with exactly the same set of possible approaches and applications.

Rule 6 also recognizes the limitations of quantitative measures, that is, at some point your ability to count things disappears, e.g., with regard to "soft" issues like morale, motivation, attitudes, engagement, and feelings. However, it is very doubtful you will call a halt to your analysis for a lack of quantitative variables to analyze. If you start with a variance, then at some point, you must uncover its root cause.

In summary, the process of analyzing a business problem consists of six basic rules that are applied over and over again. You start with the measures that are important to your company. You break that measure down into its component variables, examining relationships and variances. As you identify variances, you continue breaking down the variables at one level into the component variables at the next level. This process continues until you find something you can impact that will have the desired effect on the starting measure. Thus, you not only find solutions to your company's business problems, but you can demonstrate to all levels of the company's organization just how you are going to solve them, including their value. This is how you get buy-in.

Additional Procedural Initiatives

Additionally, there are six *procedural* rules which are for use when analyzing organizational or operating business entity deficiencies, that is, with no other knowledge than your own analytical skills and raw information about your organization. Not all attempts to solve a business or operational deficiency must start at that point. There are some simpler approaches as illustrated with these *general* rules with regard to identifying, quantifying, and then resolving the organizational business deficiencies:

Procedural Rule 1: Analyze known business problems first.

Procedural Rule 2: To identify unknown company business problems:

> a) Verify potential issues contained in company documentation or relevant industry documentation;
>
> b) If that does not reveal problems and opportunities, analyze your company's business from scratch;
>
> c) Probe your company for problems, issues, and concerns. Interview people at all levels including high performers at all levels.

Procedural Rule 3: When analyzing business problems from scratch, begin the analysis at the financial level then move through the operational levels to the functional levels.

Procedural Rule 4: When looking for industry standards to define the desired conditions,

> a) Use your company standards first, then
> b) Use industry norms and standards, then
> c) Use historical records.

Procedural Rule 5: Position and obtain support for identified solutions at whatever levels of the organization necessary. Position and obtain support at the functional level first, then position and obtain support at the operational and financial levels.

Procedural Rule 6: Take the simple ones first. You get a quick win and build momentum. Remember to celebrate failure, learn from it, and quickly move on.

Together, the six general rules for conducting an analysis from scratch and the six procedural rules for analyzing business problems provide about all the guidance you will need to successfully identify, prioritize, and solve business problems through the application of redesigned and improved process along with applied technology. These rules are consolidated for easy reference.

Common Financial Terms

Accounts Payable: This is money owed by a company for materials or services purchased. The financial reports that are available at low cost from banks and other credit reporting agencies for business firms often indicate whether or not a firm is paying its bills on time. This information is gathered from the firm's creditors and shows the amounts owed, the normal credit terms in days, and the dates the actual bills were paid (or, if overdue, how many days overdue).

Accounts Receivable: Money owed to a company for materials, goods, and/or services sold. It is important to know how well your company is collecting amounts owed to them. An analysis of accounts receivable should be made monthly in one of two ways:

1. By classifying accounts receivable in terms of the number of days bills are owed to the firm and evaluating the results. For example:

a. 0 to 30 days	$10,000
b. 31 to 60 days	$90,000
c. 61 to 90 days	$30,000
d. Over 91 days	$10,000

We might conclude that $10,000 of debts are turning bad and that "slow" collection of $30,000 is too high. A lot depends on who the customers are, how large, how complex the orders were, whether orders were shipped in whole lots or in pieces, what the terms of sale were, what incentives are given for early payments, what penalties are included for late payments, etc. Your company will help with establishing the judgment calls needed for a meaningful review.

2. By determining the average number of days all accounts receivable are outstanding. This average number is also known as the collection period. This measure can then be compared to the credit terms granted to customers by the firm or standards within the industry. Deviations from this norm are both a warning signal and a measurement of the effectiveness of your company's credit department. Also, it may be an indication of the value and/or quality of the accounts receivable. Care must be taken, however, to prevent credit policies from becoming so strict as to restrict sales – and profits.

3. To find days of sales represented by receivables:

a. Calculate receivables as a percentage of sales for the period. For example, on a year-ending statement with sales of $200,000 and accounts receivable of $50,000, the resulting accounts receivable (A/R) ratio would be 25%.

b. Apply this to the number of days in the period. In this example, 25% of 365 days equals 91.25 days. Some firms just use 30 days for a month, 90 days for a quarter, and 360 days for a year to keep the math simple. This would likely not fit a seasonal business, e.g. toys, summer wear, winter wear, travel, etc.

Accrued Expenses: similar to or same as accrued liabilities. Amounts currently owed. For instance, sometimes the end of the accounting period will come at a time not concurrent with a payroll date so that money owed to certain employees for work performed for, as example, three days. This amount could then be shown as accrued expenses – the amount will be estimated from previous payrolls. Other types of accrued expenses might be taxes, depreciation, bond interest, insurance premiums, etc.

Acid Ratio: Often called the "quick ratio" because it is a ratio comparison of the current assets (cash and cash equivalents) with current liabilities. To find the "quick ratio" divide the current assets – which may not be quickly converted to cash or cash equivalents – by the current liabilities. This is a quick indication of solvency. A 1:1 ratio means that the organization can meet its short term obligations.

Amortization: Intangible non-current assets such as patents, copyrights, goodwill, organizational costs, or leaseholds must be written off over a period of years – their useful life as a norm. They lose value over time just as do physical assets. Amortization is the accounting process of writing off such intangibles just as depreciation is the writing off of physical assets.

Assets: Everything of value owned by a firm.

Balance Sheet: A typical balance sheet shows, as of a certain point in time (date), all of the assets (everything of value owned by the firm, classified into separate categories such as cash, securities owned, accounts receivable, inventories, machinery and equipment, and buildings and land, etc.) The balance sheet also shows all of the liabilities (debts or obligations of the firm) such as accounts payable, notes payable, payroll money owed, etc. The difference between assets (what is owned) and the liabilities (what is owed) is also shown on the balance sheet as the equity or ownership capital (net worth).

Book Value: The value of the company as shown on the books as net assets – all the assets minus all liabilities. The book value is not likely to be the value of the company if it were liquidated. Book value just provides a *benchmark* for evaluating the worth of a company.

Book Value/Share of Stock: The value for each class of stock divided by the paid-in capital and surplus applicable to that class of stock.

Capitalization Ratios: The proportion of each kind of security (bonds, debentures, preferred stock, and common stock) to the total business entity. Interest on bonds and debentures usually must be paid before dividends on common stock. Excessively high ratios for bonds or debentures reduced the attractiveness of the preferred stock. Similarly, too high a preferred stock ratio reduces the attractiveness of the common stock. Here is an example:

	Computation of Values	
	Amount	Ratio
Bonds (all types)	$3000000	30%
Preferred Stock	$500000	5%
Common stock, capital surplus, and retained earnings	$6500000	65%
Total Capitalization	$10000000	100%

Generally, an industrial company will have a bond ratio of less than 25% and the common stock ratio should be as much as the total of the bond and preferred stock ratios.

Capital Surplus (aka Earnings Retained in the Business or Earned Surplus): The net assets minus the value of common and preferred stock at their par values. The Association of Independent CPAs has recommended that the term "surplus" be discontinued, and the following terms be used:

1. Paid-in-capital in excess of par. Common stock often has a no-par or low-par value (issued face value) to reduce certain taxes. The amount it is sold for originally minus the par value provides the "excess capital" paid in.

2. Retained earnings (earned surplus) are the accumulated earnings less dividends paid from the date of incorporation. If a company has heavy losses, retained earnings may be wiped out and even the original capital might be reduced.

Cash Flow Analysis: An analysis of cash received and cash disbursed to show net cash on hand or cash required for each month (or other period such as quarter or week) of the year ahead. The purpose is to ensure that the company will be able to pay current bills and obligations as well as to invest cash surpluses wisely. A cash flow analysis is also used to aid decision-makers in evaluating major alternative capital investments. In this case, the discounted cash flow for each investment may be compared. More complicated techniques, internal rate of return or MAPI, are sometimes applied to each cash flow analysis for decision making.

Collection Period: See accounts receivable. Too long a collection period may indicate:

    1. Poor controls – allowing customers to pay at their discretion;

    2. Poor marketing policies – selling to second rate customers;

    3. Poor credit policies – passing credits to companies in financial difficulties resulting in a large percentage of bad debt losses. Too short a collection period may indicate lost sales through overly stringent credit policies.

To calculate, see accounts receivable – same technique.

Compound Rate of Growth: If a firm's sales increase at 10% per year, they will not double in 10 years but rather 7.2 years. If sales doubled in 7.2 years, their compound rate of growth would be 10% meaning sales increased at 10% each year over the previous year. To find the number of years it will take for a number to double at any given rate of increase, divide 72 by the rate. For example, given a 6% rate of increase, $72 \div 5 = 12$. Therefore, it will take approximately 12 years for the original amount to double at a 6% increase per year.

Consolidated Statement of Income: See Profit and Loss Statement. "Consolidated" means the inclusion of all companies owned over 50% by the parent company unless otherwise stated.

Contribution Margin: The excess of sales over variable costs expressed as a fraction or percentage of sales. Any product or service which has a positive contribution margin contributes towards paying overhead expenses or increasing profit or both. Important Note: Often a share of *fixed* costs is arbitrarily assigned to a product which makes it appear that the product should be dropped when actually it have a positive contribution margin.

Cost of Sales, Cost of Goods Sold: The total of materials used in the manufacturing (or provisioning process), e.g., beginning inventory plus purchases not received, minus ending inventory, plus labor cost for manufacturing, plus production overhead. In retail stores, the cost of goods sold is acquisition cost of merchandise, plus transportation cost and sometimes minus any cash discounts. (Other adjustments can be made according to trade practices.) Cost of sales or cost of goods manufactured is used to show the manufacturing cost and the *gross profit* (sales minus manufacturing costs) which can then be used for comparative purposes (year over year or period to period) with all operating expenses (sales, advertising, administrative, etc.) segregated. In retail stores, sales minus cost of goods sold is usually referred to as gross margin. Gross margin also is expressed as a percentage. The formula if gross profit divided by sales.

Current Assets: All assets readily convertible into cash within one year.

Current Debt/Net Worth and Total Debt/Net Worth: These two ratios indicate the proportion of total debt and current debt to the equity (money put in by the owners including retained earnings) of the owners (stockholders). If the ratio of debt to equity is high, then the leverage is high. If leverage is too high, additional funds will likely be difficult or impossible to raise. While some "go-go" financial types say that the higher the leverage the greater the chance of gain for the owners, more conservative analysts will not invest in companies where total debt to net worth is over 100%, or net worth exceeds a certain percentage they deem proper for the particular type of business. To calculate, divide total debt or current debt by net worth.

Current Debt, Current Liabilities: This is money owed by the firm which must be paid within one year or less. Current debt is the portion of the total debt payable within one year and *includes current maturities of long-term debt.*

Current Ratio: Found by dividing current assets by current liabilities. This determines the ability of a firm to pay its short-term (less than one year) payables responsibility.

Depreciation: All allocation made on the books to record the cost of the use of an asset during as accounting period. For example, a vehicle purchased brand new for $30,000 may only be worth $24,000 at the end of the first year. The $6,000 difference ($30,000 minus $24,000) is a reduction in value and a *cost of doing business* called depreciation. Depreciation, therefore, is a true expense of doing business although it is a non-cash journal entry. Purchase of an asset can be thought of as the purchase of a "fund of usefulness" used in the operation of a business. A portion of the "fund" is consumed or expires until it has no value and must be replaced. If the vehicle mentioned above is needed to operate the business and can be used for five years, at which time it can be traded or sold for $5,000 for a new vehicle, then the depreciation cost per year is $5,000 ($30,000 original purchase price minus $5,000 sale or trade in value = $25,000 divided by five years equals $5,000 per year depreciation cost).   Depreciation is a direct charge against profit and if it is not taken, or too little is taken, profit will be overstated. Financial analysts are well advised, therefore, to investigate depreciation charges as thoroughly as possible.   Annual statements generally have footnotes indicating depreciation policies. The methods firms used in depreciating assets, whether they be on materials, machinery, buildings, etc. can make a very substantial difference in a firm's reported profit.

Earnings Per Share: This is figured by taking the profit of the company and deducting dividends on preferred stock, if any, and dividing it by the number of outstanding shares of common stock. This is a major measurement in public companies, usually shown quarterly.

EBITDA: Earnings Before Interest, Taxes, Depreciation and Amortization. EBITDA focuses on the financial outcome of operating decisions by eliminating the impact of non-operating management decisions, such as tax rates, interest expenses, and significant intangible assets. This is often referred to as cash-flowing because it indicates most actual cash outlays that indicate whether or not the organization is self-sustaining, i.e., whether or not it is burning cash. You can go for a long time with negative Net Income but a positive EBITDA although you won't impress your owners (no returns) and you probably won't get a bank loan.

Extraordinary Income (or Loss): Refers to income or losses that are unusual, i.e., non-recurring. Usually, a footnote within the financial reports will specifically identify them.

Fixed Assets: Assets such as buildings, machinery, etc., used in the business that are not intended to, nor can they be, readily converted into cash.

Fixed Assets to Net Worth: As with other "liquidity" ratios, the purpose of this ratio is to determine the firm's ability to weather periods of stress – to meet its obligations – to pay off its creditors. If the ratio is high, the firm may be unable, or at least find it difficult, to increase its long-term debt, raising additional funds with which to pay creditors and operate the business.

Note: This ratio varies considerably from industry to industry, often high in capital intensive industries. If the ratio is too low, some analysts feel that the firm might not be making enough use of the leverage provided by using the funds of others. Other analysts think that a low ratio is indicative of good management because the company can borrow and offset temporary business mistakes or adverse conditions requiring extra cash. To calculate this ratio, divide fixed assets by net worth.

Fixed Costs: These are expenses that are relatively fixed, e.g., rents, insurance, etc., in amounts regardless of production and/or sales volume as opposed to variable costs which vary in close proportion to changes in production and/or sales volume. Some costs are fixed or partially fixed under certain conditions, e.g., wages, benefits, utilities, etc. and variables under other conditions making them difficult to categorize.

Fixed Liabilities: These are typically long-term liabilities. These are debts not anticipated to be paid off in less than a year. For example, a five-year bank note or long term bonds would usually be considered a fixed liability.

Funded Debt: This is usually long term debt, e.g., bonds, notes, debentures, with specific dates at which time the loans will be paid.

Funded Debt/Net Working Capital: This ratio is used in conjunction with other liquidity ratios to determine first whether or not long or short-term debt is in proper proportion to net working capital and second, if it is not in proportion, where is it faulty. To calculate, divide funded debt by working capital.

Goodwill: If one firm acquires another and pays more for its stock than the net value of the assets, it may show the difference as goodwill. Goodwill is normally written off over a 10-year term. Accountants often look with skepticism at goodwill as corporate practices vary widely in assigning value to goodwill.

Gross Margin: Net sales minus cost of sales (same of cost of goods sold) which can be expressed as a percentage of sales or in dollars. Gross margin is the amount of dollars left from sales after the cost of goods sold has been deducted with which all other expenses (selling and administrative, or G&A, for example) can be paid, and from which the profit is realized.

Gross Revenue: Same as sales, merchandise shipped, or professional services rendered.

Income Statement: Another name for Profit and Loss (P&L) Statement.

Intangibles: The term intangibles refers to the value of non-physical assets such as trademarks, patents, goodwill, intellectual property, or franchise value. Some companies have reduced the value of intangibles to $1, others continue to assign large amounts to their value.

Inventory: Refers to stock on hand. In manufacturing firms generally there are three types of inventory: 1. raw materials, 2. work in progress including an allocation for production and other costs already in the partially finished goods, and 3. finished goods. While supplies of stationery, pens, and pencils are in an inventory of office supplies (prepaid office expense), generally the term inventory refers only to materials used in the manufacturing process or the finished goods offered for sale. The inventory value is stated at cost or market value – whichever is lower. Market value must consider obsolescence, deterioration, decline in prices, etc. in order to be a conservative valuation.

Leverage: The use of borrowed money to increase profit and hence increase the rate of return on the owners' invested capital. The debt/equity ratio (see current debt/net worth) measures the leverage. Usually, a high value of 50% is considered quite high for a firm depending on the industry. A value of zero to 20% may indicate the firm is not maximizing its growth opportunities.

Liabilities: The debts or obligations of a firm which must eventually be paid off. See current liabilities, fixed liabilities, and funded debt.

Long Term Debt: Debt that is due for a period usually greater than one year.

Marketable Securities: An asset, usually an investment of funds not needed immediately in the operation of the business which can quickly be converted into cash with a minimum of market fluctuation e.g., public equities, short term government notes, commercial paper, bonds, etc.

Net Profit: The amount of profit earned by the firm after paying all expenses, including taxes.

Net Profit/Net Sales: A measure of profitability and good management. This ratio must be high for the industry and accompanied by a stable or growing market share to be considered good. For example, 2% or 3% might be very good for a retail food chain with its high volume, provided the chain was not pricing so high as to decrease its market share. On the other hand, in a high-technology manufacturing industry, 20%-30% might be a more typical range. To calculate, divide profit by net sales.

If a firm is not earning sufficient profit on the money that the owners (stockholders) have invested in the business to pay dividends and/or put more money back into the business so that it will grow and remain competitive, then there isn't much sense in continuing the business. Many firms have as an objective a certain return on net worth. The exact figure is based on the type of business, degree of risk involved, etc., but rarely is the objective less than 8% (utilities), and often is as high a 20% or more – high risk aircraft or technology firm – or retail stores where turnover is so high that investment can be as low as in discount stores. As with profit percentages on sales, if this ratio is too high, growth may be inhibited by too high a selling price. To calculate, divide profit by net worth.

Net Profits/Net Worth (ROI): The measure of the business relative to other opportunities for investing money.

Net Sales/Inventory: A very important ratio inasmuch as comparison with other companies in the same type of business often tells a great deal about the effectiveness of management's policies and control. If inventory turnover is poor, any or all of the following may be indicated:

1. Marketing policies are poor. Too many items in the assortment were offered. Trying to be all things to all people. Not enough market research to have a "since of direction." May be selling through the wrong sales channels or to too many unprofitable customers.

2. No policies at all – allowing the customer and/or the market to dictate policy or allowing production to say to marketing "you must sell everything or anything we produce," or conversely, "you in production must produce everything our customers need" or "competition requires that we have a complete (meaning too full) product or service line."

3. Controls of the company are poor or not enforced or both. Objectives are not clearly spelled out, not known, or not followed.

Inventories that are too large:

1. Tie up money needlessly, reduce return on investment and/or require additional capital which may be better used elsewhere.

2. Often result in excessive losses because large inventories can:

    a. Increase obsolescence;

    b. Result in product deterioration;

    c. If funds are needed elsewhere or in a forced liquidation are sold at heavy markdowns.

Inventories that are too low:

1. Increase stock outages which may slow down or shut processing for lack of parts or materials and/or lose customers;

2. Increase cost of manufacturing due to small or broken lots, or excessive expenditures because of short runs.

To calculate, divide net sales by inventory.

Net Sales to Net Worth: This ratio (expressed in numbers or times rather than percentages) indicates the turnover relationship between sales and equity (ownership funds).   Generally, the higher the turnover the higher the profit is likely to be. Sometimes high turnover may indicate an under-capitalized company (which is the major cause of early failure in new businesses).   Use this ratio with other ratios to get the full meaning, e.g., current ratio, debt to net worth, etc.   To calculate, divide net sales by equity (same as net worth).

Net Working Capital: Current assets minus current liabilities (sometimes called working capital). Analysts refer to the net working capital position because it represents the excess of assets readily convertible into cash with which to pay current moneys owed.

Net Worth: The total of all assets minus all liabilities. This means the total of preferred stock, common stock, and all surplus, or, in other words, the ownership capital of the business (equity).

Notes Payable: A loan to the business usually payable on certain specified dates, on which interest is usually paid, and evidenced by a written "note." Notes can be guaranteed by collateral, an owner's personal guarantee, or merely backed by the general credit of the company.

Operating Expenses: Costs directly related to the running of the business (selling and administrative expense) but not including cost of goods (manufacturing expense) and not such things as income taxes or costs not directly related, e.g., charitable contributions, for example.

Operating Leverage: When a more than proportional increase in profit results from increase sales volume. Operating leverage is sometimes used by marketing managers as a reason to shave the selling price on large volume orders. A complete study of fixed and variable expenses, the breakeven point, etc., is generally advisable before such action is taken as well as applicable Federal law which may specifically restrict or prohibit such a cutting of prices.

Operating Profit: Profit before other income and before income taxes.

Other Assets: May be patents, goodwill, intellectual property, etc.

Other Expenses: Expenses other than those normally shown as cost of goods sold or selling, administrative, and general expenses. Accrued liabilities or small interest expenses are sometimes included in other expenses.

Other Income: May come from rents, securities owned, etc. that is income not directly related to the principal business of the firm.

Prepaid Expense: Expenses paid before all the services have been rendered. For example, insurance premiums may be paid a year in advance, and at the time the statement period was ended may have been paid for six months into the future.

Primary Earnings (per share): Dividing earnings by the number of shares outstanding plus the number that would be outstanding if all convertible securities (including stock options and warrants) were converted into common stock.

Profit: The amount left over after all operating expenses have been paid or accounted for. Often shown before taxes have been deducted.

Profit and Loss Statement: A financial summary of the operations of a company by sales, costs, expenses, income, etc. for a specified period of time – usually for three, six, nine, or twelve months, although most firms' accountants create profit and loss statements each month.

Profit Margin: Earnings before interest and taxes divided by sales and usually expressed as a percentage.

Pro Forma Statements: Income and Balance Sheet statements for future years which are part of the company's plan. They are also prepared for consideration of special plans such as mergers or new ventures.

Quick Assets: Same as the Acid Ratio. Quick assets equal current assets minus inventories.

Retained Earnings: The accumulation of earnings (not paid out in dividends) which is kept in the business for day-to-day operation and/or for expansion of the business.

Return on Equity: A very important percentage indicating the money earned (not profit) on the net worth (money put into the business or later added.) It is the same as Net Profit/Net Worth. To find, divide net profits by the company's net worth.

R.O.I.: Return on Investment. Same as Return on Equity and Net Profits/Net Worth.

Revenue: This is all the firm's income - regardless of source. Mention reconciliation between affiliates.

Sinking Fund: An accumulation of money established by setting aside a specified amount of cash at regular intervals for the purpose of providing funds at a specific future date. For example, funds may be needed to pay off a bond issue or to replace a capital asset.

Surplus: This is another way to state Capital Surplus.

Tangible Net Worth: Net Worth (as above) minus intangible items included in the assets, such as patents, goodwill, trademarks, leaseholds, intellectual property, mailing lists, organization expenses, etc.

Turnover (Inventory): The number of times per year that average inventory (in dollar value) is sold (or moved). If sales are $1,000 and the average inventory selling price is $250, the turnover is $1,000 divided by $250 or *4 times per year.*

Be Careful: In figuring inventory turnover, be sure to use either sales at *selling price* and average inventory at *selling price* or sales *at cost* (cost of goods sold) divided by average inventory *at cost.*

Turnover is best compared with turnover of companies in similar lines of business as slow turnover or fast turnover is often a characteristic of the particular type of business, i.e., slow turnover is characteristic of piano manufacturing, aged whiskey, expensive antiques, etc.

Footnotes

1. This grid is taken from Managerial Grid, by Robert Blake and Jane Mouton.

2. Robert M. McCollum, Division Manager, Fort Worth, Texas, Southwestern Bell Telephone Company, one of my best bosses whom I had the pleasure to work for twice.

3. When I was a 2nd level manager at Southwestern Bell, I was initially promoted to long distance sales manager in Dallas, then lateral transferred to St. Louis to be a product manager, then lateral transferred to Ft. Worth to lead a division staff, then lateral transferred to Dallas to gain experience on the Dallas area staff, then finally lateral transferred out into Dallas operations to be a sales manager in the banking industry which had an equipment focus. Each job gave me *substantial* business experience and exposure – which made me a top candidate for a 3rd level manager position, which I achieved the following year.

4. Improving closing skills in sales is typically a function of experience and trial and error – not just desire. It is usually a gradual process that takes several months of a high level of activity to master.

5. "Red line" time is essentially when the phone rings, an email comes in, whatever, with an urgent item or problem that must be resolved immediately. Your morning or afternoon productivity is lost to an emergency that couldn't wait.

6. Reading Suggestions: A great resource for developing a corporate value statement is a 2002 Harvard Business Review article written by well-known business author Patrick M. Lencioni, *Make Your Values Mean Something.* A great resource for developing a corporate vision is a 1996 Harvard Business Review article by well-known business authors James C. Collins and Jerry I. Porras, *Building Your Company's Vision.* Another good resource is *Balancing Individual and Organizational Values: Walking the Tightrope to Success,* by Ken Hultman.   Finally, check out *Strategic Corporate Social Responsibility: Sustainable Value Creation,* by David Chandler.

7. Reading Suggestions: There are several great books on employee engagement available anywhere business books are sold. To name a few – *The Truth About Employee Engagement,* by Patrick Lencioni, *Employee Engagement 2.0,* by Kevin Kruse, *1,001 Ways to Engage Employees,* by Bob Nelson, PhD, and *Carrots and Sticks Don't Work,* by Paul L. Marciano, PhD.

8. Taken from *Can I Count on You?,* by Mike Scott. Check out www.totallyaccountable.com.

9. Taken from the HBR article *Management Time: Who's Got the Monkey?*

10. Reading Suggestions: Some good books on building accountability into your organization's culture are *You Can Count on Me,* by Mike Scott, *The Accountability Factor,* by Oswald R. Viva & Deborah Vaughn, *What You Accept is What You Teach: Setting Standards for Employee*

Accountability, by Michael Cohen, *Winning with Accountability: The Secret Language of High-Performing Organizations*, by Henry J. Evans, and *Managing for Accountability: A Business Leader's Toolbox*, by Lynne Curry. These titles are available anywhere business books are sold.

11. Reading Suggestions: *The Speed of Trust*, by Stephen. M.R. Covey, originally published in 2008, is available anywhere business books are sold.

12. I found this trust hierarchy on the internet with an unidentified creator. It fit Covey's model completely, so I included it for a better understanding.

13. Reading Suggestions: Jerry Jellison's books on change are all very good. I recommend *Managing the Dynamics of Change* and *Overcoming Resistance: A Practical Guide to Producing Change in the Workplace*. These are available anywhere business books are sold.

14. Adapted from a Facebook posting – no documented author.

15. The Power of Positive Thinking, by Norman Vincent Peale, is available anywhere books are sold.

16. I was fortunate to be in a Vistage Chief Executive Group in Houston, Texas, led by Bill Mack, one of the nationally recognized Vistage "Super Moderators."

17. Vistage is where I heard Jerry Jellison's presentation and training on managing change in organizations. His presentation was so timely I recommended him to WTA, a national broadband

association, who featured Jerry at their next national conference.

18. The assumption here is that an executive will not necessarily perform or conduct all of these components personally but will function as a leader by delegating and utilizing available resources such as other internal, knowledgeable executives and experts along with external resources such as management and financial consultants, accountants and auditors, along with legal counsel when appropriate.

19. We bought six companies during my tenure as CEO, and each one, even after thorough vetting, had unexpected things pop up that slowed down the assimilation – although they all worked out well in the end.

20. It never ceased to amaze and frustrate me to hear of our fiber-served broadband customers leaving us for a wireless broadband service to save $5 per month or less. There is no better broadband service than underground fiber in terms of available speeds, reliability, and security.

21. I highly recommend reading *Marketing Myopia* by Theodore Levitt. It gives great insight into understanding in what "business" your organization operates, and who your competitors really are.

22. ERP is Enterprise Resource Planning systems – commonly on an SAP platform in larger organizations.

23. Direct competition consists of competitor goods and services that are similar or perhaps interchangeable with your company's goods and services.

24. Indirect competition is competition that comes from your organization's internal operations affecting the decision-making process, i.e., a decision to spend operating capital on plant expansion (or other capital-intensive activity) rather than on your organization's business initiatives. Said another way, it is reallocated budget moneys *away* from your area to *other* internal areas.
25. Quarantines early in the pandemic were 14 days which caused a great gap in our technician force.
26. The article is *The Five Deadly Business Sins*, written by Peter Drucker, and published in the Wall Street Journal on Thursday, October 23, 1993. It is a great article.
27. Corporate-wide, departmental, divisional, product or service – whatever fits the scope of the Plan.

Dave Osborn

For over 17 years Dave Osborn was Chief Executive Officer of the VTX1 Companies headquartered in Raymondville, Texas, and, through strategic plans, organic growth, and acquisitions, increased the company revenues 400%. The VTX1 Companies operate broadband internet, voice, and fiber transport lines of business within a 47,500 square mile service area in South and Central Texas. Under Mr. Osborn's vision and leadership, the VTX1 Companies grew from around 5,200 customers to over 42,000 customers and are now the second largest independent broadband company in Texas.

Dave began his distinguished 52½ year career with Southwestern Bell in Dallas and progressed through positions of increasing responsibility in Dallas, St. Louis, Ft. Worth, Kansas City, Houston, concluding as an executive at AT&T company headquarters at Morristown, New Jersey. Following that, he had many years' experience ranging from startups to large telecom and computer network equipment manufacturers culminating in his final CEO position.

Dave was considered a turnaround and strategic planning expert within the industry.

During his career, Dave served as a Board Member and Treasurer for the *Texas Telephone Association (TTA)* and was also a Board Member of the *Western Telecommunications Alliance (WTA)* and the *Texas State Telecommunications Cooperative (TSTCI)*. Mr. Osborn was also a long time member of the Board of Directors for the *Texas Lone Star Network (TLSN)* and the Houston-South Texas *Better Business Bureau (BBB)* and served as the Bureau's 2016-2018 Board Chair.

Dave received recognition over the years for his many contributions to the telecommunications industry, including the Texas Telephone Association's prestigious *Neville Haynes Award* for 2013 and 2022 as well as the National Telephone Cooperative Association's *Telecom Executive* Certificate.

Dave holds a Bachelor of Science Degree from Stephen F. Austin State University in Nacogdoches, Texas, and a Masters of Business Administration from Texas Christian University in Ft. Worth, Texas.

Dave enjoys South Texas bird hunting and bay fishing and is an avid grill master. Additionally, Dave is a bluegrass music fan and enjoys playing the piano, guitar, bass, and five-string banjo. Also, one of Mr. Osborn's favorite pastimes is coastal sailing, and he holds both U.S. and International coastal sailing certifications.

Dave resides in Harlingen, Texas, with his wife Marilyn and rescue dog Piper. Two adult children and two grandsons reside in the greater Houston area.